About the Author

Karen Christensen has been writing about the environment since 1989. Her books have been published in Germany, France, and China as well as the United States and Britain. She is senior editor of the *International Encyclopedia of Women and Sports* (Macmillan Reference 2000) and co-editor of the *Encyclopedia of World Sport* (Oxford 1999). Her other books include the *Global Village Companion* and the children's picture book *Rachel's Roses*.

Karen has been a prominent speaker on women's issues for the Green Party and helped found the Women's Environmental network and Ecological Design Association. She has appeared on BBC, Central Television, and Discovery Channel programmes, as well as giving dozens of radio interviews in the UK and United States. She lectures on environmental issues, most recently at the well-known American health spa, Canyon Ranch in the Berkshires.

Karen also runs a publishing business that specialises in global information and is active in local politics and the Slow Food Movement.

Eco Living

Eco Living

A Handbook for the 21st Century

Karen Christensen

PIATKUS

Contents

Acknowledgements

Eco Living is a compendium of ideas and insights from people and organisations around the world, many of whom have helped me before. Among them are the Women's Environmental Network, Worldwatch Institute, Global Action Plan, Going for Green and John Elkington and Julia Hailes of SustainAbility. Brian Price, who helped, once again, with the chemistry I've long forgotten, and Helen Carey, director of the Women's Institute, have been a source of ideas and much enthusiasm. The work of the Union of Concerned Scientists in Cambridge, Massachusetts, has helped me sort out the relative impact of choices we make, and US architect and designer William McDonough and energy experts Amory and Hunter Lovins, of the Rocky Mountain Institute, have inspired me to believe that we can do much more than simply reduce pollution. Freelancers Pam Dix and Laura Manchester helped with research and editing, and at Piatkus Books I want to thank Gill Bailey, Melissa Harrison, Jana Sommerlad, Claire Richardson and Elizabeth Hutchins. And I am deeply grateful to readers who have written to share their stories with me and to Jonathon Porritt for his foreword.

My husband David says I should write a book about French cooking or tropical vacations next time, since he's the one who has to live with my obsessions. This book is dedicated to him and to my children, Tom and Rachel, with love and gratitude.

Foreword

by Jonathon Porritt

Karen Christensen's first book, the predecessor of *Eco Living*, came out in 1989. A huge amount has changed during that time and all sorts of things that were still considered pretty wacky in those days are now taken for granted – have become fashionable even. No one now disputes that we all need to be doing more to protect the environment, and many of the solutions to those problems are rapidly becoming mainstream.

Just consider the standing of organic food in society today, for instance. Having once been dismissed by farmers, retailers and most politicians as an irrelevant niche market catering for health freaks and tree-huggers, it's now seen as the single most important antidote to the totally discredited model of post-war intensive farming. Sales of organic food in the UK are now growing by more than 40 per cent a year.

The hunger for user-friendly down-to-Earth advice about what each of us can do to play our part in this process is greater than ever. For me, *Eco Living* stands out as one of the best guidebooks available today, not least because it is about a lot more than 'green consumerism'. Individual lifestyle choices, arising out of an acceptance of personal responsibility for those parts of our lives that we can directly control, are set in a much broader social, political and philosophical context. As Karen says, 'This is not a green consumer guide. It's about better living, not better buying.' And better living means thinking of ourselves primarily as citizens (be it of our local community or of planet Earth itself) and only after that as consumers.

Even as we reduce our energy consumption, buy more organic produce and eliminate the last of those chemicals we might once have used in the garden, we must not ignore the political side: the letter-writing, the joining with others in local or national campaigns, the encouraging of best practice wherever we find it, and so on.

Both aspects of 'eco living' – the practical and the political – are essential. Each depends on the other. And that's very much where this book is coming from.

It's only through that combination that we can gradually bring our own way of life (and ultimately the way of life of each and every individual nation state) into line with the natural rhythm and cycles of nature. Our trajectory as a species cuts directly across those natural systems, wasting, polluting, poisoning, systematically liquidating the 'natural capital' on which we depend as utterly as every other species. Realigning that trajectory, by completely reconceptualising what progress and development really mean, is the greatest challenge we now face.

So we have still got a very long way to go. But as many have pointed out before, the journey of a thousand miles starts with a single step – and one of the things that I like best about *Eco Living* is that (unlike many books) it won't make concerned and committed people feel inadequate or paralysed by guilt! Though it reminds me of endless shortcomings in my own lifestyle (busy green activists are often far from the paragons of environmental virtue that they might aspire to be – and no one aspires more than I do!), it encourages rather than turns me off.

As Karen says, there's no point being 'grim and miserable' if you are seeking a greener way of life and a greener home. At its simplest (but most easily overlooked) level, environmentalism is all about celebrating the gift of life – life writ large, that is, not just the human end of it. Better by far to be celebrating that gift wreathed in smiles than permanently garbed in sackcloth and ashes – to celebrate, for instance, the joy of good fresh food rather than becoming obsessed by what we should or shouldn't be eating.

Karen declares that her secret to happiness is 'not getting more but wanting less'. I suspect that we are both still working away at that secret. *Eco Living* is about work in progress, not about some revealed truth from a distant green guru – and it is all the more useful and enjoyable for it.

Jonathon Porritt

January 2000

Introduction

Most worthy authors of environmental books don't realise how much most people have to think about: daycare, the company's plan to relocate, finding a date, doing taxes. They bombard us with statistics and indigestible lists of advice, and mix good practical suggestions with completely nutty ideas ('Write small so you use less paper'). They think we have endless time and money to devote to the cause. But in between figuring out how to afford a new suit or find time to go to the gym, we want to know where our choices can have the greatest environmental impact. And we want environmental thinking to contribute to a sense of well-being and balance in our lives, not to unhinge us altogether!

What is eco living? It's a way of describing twenty-first-century living, which at its best will mean going about our lives in a sustainable way that also makes sense in terms of practical demands we all face. Eco living isn't a hobby, or a part-time job, but a perspective that will bring a myriad of positive changes to the world we live in.

This book offers an easy-to-use overview of a great variety of topics – some standard eco thinking and others ideas that are a bit more daring. The issues tackled range from the hormone disruption caused by household plastics to the over-exploitation of our oceans, global warming and the growing chemical burden on us and on the environment. Yet this is a practical book, tested amidst the rush and jumble of modern family life. *Eco Living* goes far beyond recycling – an important but yawn-provoking subject

– to cover leisure and holidays, gardening in the city and preserving our memories. Packing everything you need to know about eco living into 200 pages has been one of the hardest jobs of my life! There are chapters on 'Body Care' and 'What You Wear' and a chapter explaining how new technologies, from computer monitors to mobile phones and online auctions, affect our lives and the environment.

Decide what matters to you most. You don't have to change cleaning products, spend more time in natural light and start cycling to work all at once! Identify two or three changes that will make a big difference. Where do you use the most water, or paper, or energy? And don't try to do too much, too soon. No matter how small the beginning, it is better to do something than nothing.

Eco Living is not focused on the usual 'eco efficiency', which involves doing things in ways that pollute *less*. Instead, I've tried to explain some of the big ideas being discussed today for moving our society towards methods and products that will not pollute *at all*. This truly ecological model is far more ambitious, but ultimately more hopeful. We need to turn every system – manufacturing, education, household – into one that is sustainable by figuring out ways to do things that create *no* pollution, just like Nature's systems, in which everything has a use. The most creative environmental thinkers are working in this direction, and I find it uplifting to think that we can, by working together and encouraging best practice, turn things round.

I see eco living as a way of clarifying the things that really matter to me, so I can concentrate my efforts where they count. Many of the tips in the book can also be downloaded from our website (iwww.EcoLiving.com), where they are coded to show how much time they take, how much money they cost and how much impact they have.

>Basics for Buying

One aspect of eco living is becoming a green consumer. But some 'green' products are plain silly – do you really need a £25 gadget to test whether your microwave is leaking? Some don't take account of basic eco principles – is it worth having recycled drinking glasses shipped all the way from South Africa? But it's great to see more eco products around, and one of my goals is to help you judge what's good and what's not.

- *Do* take special care over major purchases like buying a car or refrigerator, or installing a new roof or a heating system. *Don't* agonise over a plastic bag!
- Be a leader: if you have the money, you can make a big difference by being among the first to adopt a new technology, such as a solar water heater or an electric car.
- Watch your weight: anything heavy takes a lot of energy to ship.
- Imitate nature: choose products and methods made from natural materials that can be reused or that will biodegrade.
- Buy things that have already had one owner.
- Share tools, exotic cookware, even a car, with friends or neighbours.
- If in doubt, choose the cheapest method. It's likely to be eco friendly.
- Use things as long as possible and buy the best replacement you can find.
- Follow William Morris's rule: 'Have nothing in your houses that you do not know to be useful, or believe to be beautiful.'

I'm convinced that the key to a sustainable future lies not in technological progress but in our human connections, our sense of community and our love for the natural world. I'd love to hear your ideas and suggestions. Please write to me – karen@berkshirepublishing.com – or
c/o Piatkus Books, 5 Windmill Street, London W1P 1HF.
You'll also find updates at www.iEcoLiving.com, along with downloadable tips sheets and the latest resource links.

Food and Drink

Some experts think that home cooking will disappear during this century and that traditional foods and techniques will be preserved only in the 'museum' of restaurant kitchens. I prefer to listen to the many who share my belief that the kitchen is the centre of our homes, a place where we should find comfort, sustenance and companionship.

Eating is the most intimate activity we engage in in public and eating together is fundamental to almost every human group. Food is a source of pleasure and comfort, of nutrition and variety, and growing and preparing food can be deeply satisfying. But today we hear continually about the dangers of eating, from fat and cholesterol, pesticides and dioxins to 'Frankenfoods' – genetically modified plants and animals. Also, we have become reliant on convenience food which we can prepare and eat quickly as we rush through our busy lives. As we consider the quality of life we want, however, our priorities may change. The time-saving nature of convenience products is in fact often illusory. Natural rice needs to cook for longer than the instant variety, but its preparation requires no more of your time. Cooking and sharing a meal take more time than sticking individual frozen pizzas into the microwave, but eating together plays a vital role in any human group, and shared preparation is both creative and pleasurable.

Restoring a positive relationship to food and a healthy, sustainable system of growing and processing it is a basic step in creating a sustainable world. Fortunately, the changes that will improve your health, make you feel more confident about the food you serve and, most important of all, give you and your friends and family greater pleasure in eating together will also benefit the environment.

Q Many recent studies show that highly coloured foods – dark green, orange, red – contain more vitamins and other beneficial components. Plan meals with a colour palette more Gauguin than Monet!

Local, Organic, Reasonable

Wandering around a small farmers' market in Santa Barbara, California, above a pile of gleaming fresh lemons nested in a basket with their leaves still on them, I spotted a sign that has for years been my basic food rule: 'Local, organic, reasonable.'

When I say 'local' I mean food that has been grown and produced somewhere near my home (perhaps even in my own garden), because there are important environmental and health benefits to eating locally. In Britain, where many smaller farmers are in dire straits, it's important to the national economy, too, that we begin to reconnect with our food heritage by eating food grown in our own regions, in our soil. Seasonality – strawberries in June, plums in September – is going to be a hallmark of great twenty-first-century eating and it will encourage us to look to homegrown foods.

In addition, I look for 'organic' food – food grown using animal and plant manures, crop rotations, biological pest control and mechanical weeding.

Finally, I think eating should be 'reasonable'. I don't think it's necessary to be fanatical about food, and we should weigh the time and money we have available against the various issues we want to take account of when we buy and cook.

Food production and transportation have a huge impact on the environment. What we buy and cook and choose in restaurants affects natural ecosystems in numerous ways. The route from farm to table is extremely complex – using all kinds of methods of preserving, processing and shipping food around the world. In the UK the cost of processing, storing and distributing food comes to over 50 per cent of the total food bill. While processing is not a bad thing – people have preserved and stored food for thousands of years – these costs reflect energy and resource use that contributes to global warming, air and water pollution and damage to ecosystems.

Q There used to be over 6,000 varieties of apple in Britain, with favourites in each region. Now, supermarkets sell two or three varieties, most of them from abroad.

Since the 1940s, when widespread pesticide use began, crop losses to insects have steadily increased because insects develop resistance to chemicals very quickly. Even conventional growers are cutting back on chemical use, with integrated pest management (IPM), which uses a portfolio of methods to control – not necessarily eradicate – crop loss.

Male sperm counts in the US and Europe have fallen by 50 per cent since the 1930s. One explanation for this decline in male fertility – and also for girls' earlier menstruation and sexual development and for the growing rate of breast and prostrate cancer – is that all of us are consuming or being exposed to the female hormone oestrogen or to chemicals that mimic it. The sources of the hormone include meat, where hormones are used as growth promoters, and the use of pesticides which appear to mimic oestrogen.

Because the Earth's population is still growing, and because we consume too much protein, the severity of nitrate contamination is expected to grow in the decades ahead. This results in ground-level ozone pollution, crop damage, forest die-back and damage to coastal fisheries from algal blooms, the so-called 'red and brown tides'.

The solution is organic and IPM farming techniques and better control of chemical fertilisers. It's also vital to return animal manures to the soil rather than dumping them. At present, about 70 per cent of the organic food sold in the UK comes from abroad because there are insufficient domestic supplies.

Q A Danish study found that men whose food was more than 50 per cent organic had sperm counts more than twice the average. *(See also Chapter 4, page 47.)*

>For your Health and the Planet's

- Eat a wide variety of foods and food varieties, including plenty of wholefoods, fruit and vegetables, and reduce your intake of animal products.
- Buy foods from close to home and those grown organically or by IPM methods.
- Buy foods in season and with simple packaging.

The Most Important Foods to Buy Organic
- baby foods
- anything containing fat (milk, butter)
- peanuts and peanut butter
- rice

TIPS: FOR FOOD AND DRINK
- Beware of perfect looking produce.
- Buy domestically grown produce in season – these generally contain fewer pesticide residues.
- Grow your own food.
- Wash all produce in plain water or a mild solution of biodegradable washing-up liquid and water.
- Peel non-organic produce to remove surface residues completely.
- Press for comprehensive labelling of fresh fruit and vegetables.

- strawberries
- breakfast cereals
- milk
- corn
- bananas
- apples

>Promoting Biodiversity

- Shop locally and buy local produce. Sources include wholefood shops and co-ops, city farms, box schemes, community supported agriculture (CSA), farmers' markets and pick your own.
- Grow some of your own food.
- Eat seasonally.
- Buy a variety of fruit and vegetables, including heritage varieties.
- Attend an apple tasting of local and old varieties such as Slack my Girdle and Ellison's Orange apples, or pick apples from an old orchard.
- Buy white eggs if brown are common, to encourage farms to raise more than one species of chicken.
- Order meat from a farmer who raises rare old breeds.
- Buy bread that contains many grains.
- In your garden, plant old roses and open-pollinated seeds.
- Serve traditional drinks: scrumpy, perry, country wines.
- Eat wild plants such as nettle and elderberries, and make traditional hedgerow drinks like sloe gin.

GM Foods

People have been selecting crops based on their genetic traits for thousands of years. Civilisations would never have arisen without this selective breeding, which provided people with productive staple crops like wheat, barley and rice. What has happened in recent years is that companies are beginning to figure out ways to alter genes in labs – to engineer life itself.

Much food research is focused on improving corporate profits, so it's no surprise that the GM developments we've seen to date have emphasised how to spend less and grow or produce more. It's no wonder people have revolted against the imposition of these new foods without adequate testing and without what seems to many observers a blatant disregard for public opinion or the consumers' right to know what they are buying and eating. As John Elkington and Julia Hailes say in their New Foods Guide, 'Consumers have been exposed to the "risks" without getting any of the benefits ... producers and retailers will need to think about how to pass a significant share of the benefits on to consumers.'

Q Recent research found that GM soya contains some 13 per cent fewer beneficial phytoestrogens than non-GM soya.

GM foods may well be part of the food future – the biotech industry is a huge global player – and there are some conceivable health and environmental benefits to be gained. What's crucial, ecologically speaking, is that extensive testing is done on any potential product and that consumers are given full information about what's on offer.

Future foods are also likely to have 'functional' components – they will be designed to make us sleep better or fight cancer. But from the ecological point of view, what counts is that we have adequate, balanced diets with plenty of organic wholefoods. From a social point of view, what counts is that we eat together, with pleasure, and without fear of imposed technologies that may threaten our health and the health of our world.

Meat and Fish

Vegetarianism is often considered essential to being green, but there is much to be said for rearing animals as part of sustainable agriculture. Virtually all cultures throughout history have used animals for food, in the form of milk, blood and meat, and traditional farming methods depend on animal manures. 'Mixed farming' creates a neat ecological cycle: animals graze fallow land and eat scraps which would otherwise be wasted (free-range chickens do even more: they eat large numbers of pests), and provide manure to fertilise the next crop. Sheep and goats are crucial in many societies, producing milk, meat and leather for clothing from land which is unsuitable for farming.

The commercial 'need' to produce meat cheaply was, however, the primary cause of BSE ('mad cow disease'). Modern meat rearing has also contributed to the rise of superbugs resistant to antibiotics. Large-scale factory farming uses antibiotics routinely in animal feed, not to fight disease but to fatten animals. This forces animals to grow unnaturally fast and contributes to the growing problem of drug-resistant bacteria.

In addition, more than half the world's grain harvest, much of it grown in developing countries, goes to feed livestock. This is an inexcusable waste of food. Most environmentalists therefore promote what is called 'eating low on the food chain'. To produce 1lb of beef requires 16lb of grain, as well as a considerable input of water; this concentration of protein is expensive and inefficient and also concentrates pesticides found in the grain or other feed. Pork is more efficient, requiring 6lb of feed to produce 1lb of meat, and the rate for broiler chickens and eggs is about three to one.

Traditional cuisines in most parts of the world, including Europe, use meat primarily as a seasoning or special treat and many cuisines that are becoming more popular in Britain use little or no meat. This has helped to break the 'meat and two veg' routine for many of us.

Veganism means eating no animal products whatsoever. This is a demanding choice because you eliminate great instant foods like eggs and cheese, but there are many wonderful vegan dishes that anyone would enjoy – consult almost any Asian cookbook for ideas.

Vegetarians and vegans have substantially lower rates of heart disease and cancer, lower blood pressure and cholesterol levels, and tend to be slimmer than meat eaters. It has been claimed that they do not get enough protein, but although this is true of many people in the Third World, in the West we get more than enough protein without eating meat or soya substitutes. Premature ageing and degenerative diseases have even been associated with eating too much protein.

For those of us who love meat, it is now possible to get meat from animals raised without growth promoters and hormones, and without additives. The RSPCA's meat monitoring scheme and the Freedom Food label ban antibiotic growth promoters. Some suppliers sell meat from rare breeds, which means that you can promote biodiversity while you grill your pork chops. These old-fashioned meats, from Sovay sheep to Old Gloucester pigs, are expensive but delicious. If you are buying from the supermarket, lamb is probably a better bet than other commercially reared meat, because sheep are primarily range animals, not stock fed with grain.

Fish is good for us, but fishing is taking a heavy toll on our oceans and inland fisheries. Most fisheries are being exploited and many once abundant sources are in essence extinct. This is because of fishing methods as well as consumption patterns. The result is long-term and even permanent damage to ecosystems.

Another result of overfishing is hunger, because fish are a critical protein source for at least 1 billion people, most of them in Africa and Asia. Some experts recommend that we eat only farm-raised fish until global fishing is properly regulated. Look for the Marine Stewardship Council fish certification logo and the Turtle-Safe Shrimp mark and do not eat swordfish, which is endangered. Check the Sea Web's website for up-to-date information on endangered fish (*see Resources*).

Animal Welfare or Animal Rights?

The terms animal welfare and animal rights are often used interchangeably, however, they look at the treatment of animals from somewhat different perspectives. Those concerned with animal welfare believe in humane treatment, but are not opposed to using animals to serve or feed human beings, whereas, for an animal rights activist the sight of a horse pulling a plough or the use of milk protein in a shampoo, not to mention a plate of steak and chips, is anathema.

To my mind, the connection between the treatment of animals and damage to the environment is both practical and ethical. Practically, intensive industrialised farming practices hurt both animals and the Earth. Ethically, human attitudes that value the non-human material world – flora, fauna and natural resources of all kinds – simply as commodities to be used and discarded are unacceptable.

Traditional cultures did not sentimentalise animals but recognised them as necessary co-inhabitants of the Earth and often had rituals surroundings the process of hunting and butchering. Gratuitous cruelty to animals is frowned on in most cultures.

There is some debate about whether animal welfare is an essential green issue. It is a more central environmental issue in Britain than it is in Italy, for instance, and the British insistence that to be green a product has to be certified cruelty-free has caused much concern. However, most people agree that animal testing of cosmetics and other non-essentials should be brought to an end world-wide, and most concerned consumers are looking for alternatives for medical testing as well *(see also Chapter 2)*.

Food Safety

Three out of five British chickens are contaminated with food poisoning bacteria. The number or reported food poisoning cases continues to rise, with an annual incidence of some 1 million cases of salmonella or *E. coli* 0157 in recent years. Infection has spread rapidly because of intensive rearing and modern slaughtering methods, which are designed to produce cheap food for a large market. Food-borne diseases are difficult to trace, because food production is much more centralised than in the past.

Another negative aspect of centralisation is the travel time involved in shipping the food from point A to point B. Trucks not only pollute our air but must also keep the food cold in order to protect it from contamination. With hundreds of packages lying on top of one another, the potential for contamination to spread is considerable. And as busy consumers, we demand that foods be brought to us in a huge volume in order to save costs and decrease the amount of time we spend shopping.

Consumers have also grown to expect certain types of food all year long, whether in season or not. Shipping food items is a problem in itself, but when these items are coming from other countries we cannot be sure about their procedures against food contamination.

Industry food safety experts concentrate on ways to destroy pathogens, from irradiation to chemical and hydrostatic pressure treatments. One even recommends that consumers spray produce with a hydrogen peroxide solution before washing it! In contrast, the ecological approach is to buy food that has been raised and produced with care, to buy local food, eat less meat and more fresh unprocessed food, and make simple changes that can help to reduce the number of outbreaks of food-borne illnesses.

The most important step to take to protect yourself from pathogens that can make you sick is to wash your hands, especially before eating. Food safety experts recommend that you wash for at least 20 seconds. It doesn't matter if the water is warm or cold, and ordinary hand soap is just as effective as anti-bacterial soap. Scrubbing under your nails is also a good idea.

As for preparing the food itself, some experts recommend wooden boards, while others prefer plastic. A well-publicised US study showed that, contrary to expectation, wooden chopping boards were safer than plastic. Almost 100 per cent of the bacteria on the wooden boards died, while in some cases bacteria multiplied on the plastic boards. But the simple solution is to keep several chopping boards: one for meat, another for vegetables and fruit (especially those that will be eaten raw) and another for bread. (I also keep a small board for garlic and onions.)

TIPS: FOR SAFE EATING

- Buy fresh and eat quickly.
- Refrigerate at less than 5°C.
- Defrost frozen foods in the refrigerator, cold water or the microwave. If you use cold water, it should be changed every hour.
- Marinate in the refrigerator only. Red meat should be marinated for three to five hours only and chicken for one to two hours.
- Do not brown or partially cook meat to finish later.
- Turn your meat while in the oven to ensure even cooking.
- Use a thermometer to test your meat before removing it from the oven. (Best taste may conflict with safety advice. For example, pork is safe, pink but moist, at 150°F (trichinosis is killed at 137°F), but is usually cooked to 160° F. Ground beef should be cooked to at least 160°F, while roasts and chops are safe at 145°F. Check with MAFF for current recommendations. *See Resources*.)
- Never reuse bags, foil, etc. that have touched raw meat or fish.
- Seafood should smell clean and mild – a strong 'fishy' smell is a warning.
- Avoid buying fresh and frozen seafood that is found in the same freezer. Buy frozen foods that are below the frost line and close to the bottom of the freezer.
- Choose vegetarian sushi or sushi with cooked fish if you're on the run. Sushi with raw fish is something to enjoy only when you know and trust the proprietor. Low-fat fish from the ocean is safest.
- Do not keep cut or cooked produce at room temperature for more than two hours.
- Do not buy bruised produce.
- Wash cutting boards with soap and hot water or run them through the dishwasher after each use. Switch to dishcloths that can be changed daily and laundered. If you use a sponge, sanitise it by laundering or by microwaving for one minute.
- Keep a hand towel for hands and a tea towel for the dishes.
- Always rinse the detergent off your dishes.

Pure Water

Most of the 700 or so known chemical contaminants in public drinking water are not detectable to the nose or eye, but many scientists and water authorities discourage home water filters because of the danger of bacterial growth. They point out that the standard of public water supplies in England and Wales is high, but admit nitrates are a growing problem. There are also potential cancer-causing disinfectant byproducts (DBPs) in water supplies; these include trihalomethanes, which are formed when chlorine reacts with organic matter such as decaying leaves.

If you use ordinary tap water, run cold water for cooking and drinking, and flush the pipes with cold water for several minutes first thing in the morning. If your water smells of chlorine, you can leave it in an uncovered container in the fridge overnight to let most of the chlorine vaporise.

Bottled waters may be pleasant, but they are bad news for the environment because of the energy used in processing and transporting them. Tests show that bottled water is no more pure than water from your tap – and it's sometimes less safe. If you must buy water, choose large glass bottles (water bottled in plastic absorbs a certain quantity of possibly carcinogenic polymers) and recycle them. If you like to carry water, reuse a glass bottle or buy a good-quality water bottle at an outdoor sports shop and refill it often.

The purest water comes from a distiller or from a reverse osmosis unit used in conjunction with a carbon pre-filter. Before deciding to use a filter you should get an analysis of your local water supply from the local water authority and insist on having laboratory test results from the supplier if you are buying an expensive system. Filtering drinking water does not remove all impurities, but can provide a safer, more palatable beverage at a reasonable price. If you use a plastic jug, change the disposable filter monthly; if overused, this can release heavy metals and possibly bacteria back into the water. A plumbed-in system is cheaper in the long run and has fewer disposable parts.

Saving Water in the Kitchen
- Use a dishwasher: running full loads on an economy cycle uses less water than washing all those dishes by hand.
- Minimise your rinsing plates for the dishwasher and bottles for recycling: just remove the carcasses.

>Coffee and Tea

Coffee and tea are staple drinks throughout most of the world. It's more ecological to drink British-grown herbal tea, but few people are willing to give up their favourite beverages, so let's look at how to encourage fair trade and sound agricultural practices.

Organically grown coffee is the ecological choice and will not only protect worker safety but also safeguard a vital habitat for migrating birds. Traditionally, coffee was grown under a canopy of trees that provided a home for diverse species, but newer industrial production of coffee relies on 'sun cultivation', which produces biological deserts. Sun cultivation systems give a higher yield, and more profits, but require more chemicals and dramatically affect biodiversity. You can have a direct influence by asking for organic shade-grown beans, which coffee connoisseurs consider far superior in flavour to the industrial product.

Organic tea is also becoming available, along with a variety of international drinks. Herbal teas are wonderful, too, but I'm doubtful that they offer all the health benefits claimed by many companies. You can make your own – it's easy to grow mint and chamomile, for example, which can be brewed fresh or dried (use an ordinary teapot – I keep a separate one for herbal teas).

Ordinary tea, from the tea plant that originated in India, contains a range of tannins, which are antioxidants, and researchers are analysing their potential health benefits. Studies suggest that Japanese green tea, made from the same tea plant as standard black tea, but dried rather than fermented, helps protect against cancer and other ills.

For good health, drink smaller amounts of higher quality, more expensive tea and coffee.

>Wines and Beers

While drinking organic beer and wine doesn't have the same potential for saving habitats, it is similarly important. Making the connection between ecological agricultural methods and great taste is one of the crucial developments of the last few years. Flavour is always relevant and organic producers now offer drinks that are competitive and reasonable, although you will pay a bit more because of the higher costs involved in organic production.

Locally brewed beer is the best eco-choice because there are virtually no transport costs. If you're lucky you might even be able to return your bottles. Bottles of wine are heavy and there are lots of 'food miles' in wine from Australia, Chile or even France.

Pots and Pans

The best cookware is expensive, but lasts for ever. Also, it will encourage you to cook because it's a pleasure to use. Good cookware conducts heat evenly so food doesn't stick or burn, it's reasonably easy to clean and the lids seal well.

There are a few health issues to keep in mind when you choose cookware. Trace amounts of nickel, a toxic metal, are found in acidic foods cooked in stainless steel and some health experts advise against refrigerating food in stainless steel. A far greater concern is aluminium, which has been associated with a number of brain disorders – I'm even cautious about the cast aluminium some expensive pans are made from. Also, don't buy pans with non-stick coatings, which release toxic fumes if overheated.

Glass is a most inert – and therefore safe – material and is fine for baking, but it doesn't conduct heat well. My favourite pans are enamelled cast iron (like Le Creuset) and I like rustic uncoated cast iron, too, because it's cheap, durable and doesn't stick. Another advantage is that your food will gain some iron from the pans, which nutritionists say is as easily absorbed as the iron in beef.

Microwaves and Other Ways to Cook

I have come to appreciate microwaves as a kitchen tool and as an energy saver. They are good for steaming vegetables and fish and for melting butter or chocolate. But their best use is heating a single dish so you don't have to use the oven or a lengthy period on the cooker.

A microwave uses only a fraction of the energy required by other cooking appliances. If you're reheating homemade dishes rather than using pre-packed food, they are a good eco-choice.

Cooking in the oven uses more energy than any other method. A toaster oven is a good alternative, and some casseroles and even jacket potatoes can be done on the cooker. Gas is preferred by serious cooks and is cheaper to use – thus more energy efficient. I'm sorry to say that Agas are not the cooker of choice in an ecological home and I was appalled to hear that some people with Agas use air conditioning to keep their kitchens cool in summer!

Appliances

Chest freezers are more efficient than upright models, though less convenient to use. If you have a freezer, defrost regularly and try to keep it full. Keeping it outside, in a garage or cellar, cuts energy costs, or put foil on the wall behind it to reflect waste heat into the room.

TIPS: FOR ENERGY SAVING IN THE KITCHEN

- Use a microwave to heat and reheat.
- Try wearing an apron, to cut down on laundry.
- Use an automatic switch-off electric kettle and heat only as much water as you need.
- Scale deposits will make your kettle less efficient, so clean with a strong vinegar solution from time to time.
- Put extra boiling water from the kettle into a Thermos for later or use it to start soaking a pan of beans.
- Improve your health and save energy by eating more raw food, salads and fresh fruit.
- Cover cooking pots to cut cooking time.
- Let the fire fit the pan: a flame licking up the side of a small saucepan is wasted.
- Don't turn the whole grill on for a single piece of toast – use a toaster.
- Fill the oven – bake a pan of apples on the lower shelf while a nut loaf – or joint of beef – is cooking higher up.
- Use a pressure cooker (stainless steel rather than aluminium) to cut cooking time drastically.
- Cut vegetables, including potatoes, into small pieces – they'll cook much more quickly.
- Allow dishes cook in their own heat – bring soup or spaghetti sauce to the boil, then turn off the flame and allow the pan to stand rather than simmer for a couple of hours.
- Use a tiered steamer to cook several types of vegetable at once.

Dishwashers save time for a large family and certainly keep the kitchen a lot tidier, but there are some arguments against having one. They require strong detergents (read the warning label) and use large amounts of hot water as well as considerable amounts of energy for drying. On the other hand, run on an economy cycle with full loads, a dishwasher can use less water than hand washing. If you use a dishwasher, look out for a phosphate- and chlorine-free washing powder and cut the amount you use to a minimum. Choose the economy setting and turn the machine off when it gets to the dry cycle – open the door and pull the racks out to air dry.

Refrigerators will be more efficient if you keep the seals clean and hoover the metal fins on the back regularly. If you're using a fridge that is more than five years old, consider a new energy-saving, frost-free model. Ensure your old fridge is recycled – many fridges contain ozone-damaging CFCs.

Home Cooking

Native cuisine around the world developed in modest family kitchens, where meals were produced from the least expensive and most abundant local foods. Nowadays an increasing number of British meals are eaten out of the home, at snack bars and cafés, pubs and restaurants. In environmental terms, this is a mixed blessing. Restaurant eating can be a good thing, as restaurants purchase foods in bulk (saving packaging) and prepare foods in large quantities (saving energy). But many restaurants, even expensive ones, serve pre-packaged and processed foods.

Fast-food restaurants are criticised by environmentalists, food and labour activists for their contribution to the destruction of tropical rainforests and loss of biological diversity, for their unfair treatment of employees, for the huge amounts of plastic and paper waste they add to the disposal stream and for the unhealthy food they sell. But the fact is that time is at a premium, and fast foods *are* fast – and cheap. People need genuine alternatives that are healthy and quick, as well as a taste for better food. Traditional fast foods were street foods sold by individuals as a way to earn a living. These foods made use of local, seasonal ingredients and had real character.

In ecological terms, buying a takeaway from a locally owned restaurant is a better choice than the kind of hamburger meal you could eat in any city. It's also a good idea to lay in a supply of wholesome, non-perishable and almost-instant food. I generally avoid tinned foods because of excessive processing and the energy cost of shipping heavy goods, but a few tins – good soups and beans and tuna fish – make a good addition to the impromptu meal shelf.

Alternatively, join Slow Food, an international movement – active in 35 countries worldwide – with over 60,000 members who care about food, culture, and conviviality. Slow Food aims to link gastronomy with ecology. Each local chapter, a convivium, holds tastings, dinners, visits to artisan food producers and food fairs, and serves as a grassroots connection between the consumer and organic farmers and artisan food producers. (*See Resources for more information.*)

TIPS: FOR HOME COOKING

- Stock your pantry with staples that last.
- Buy in bulk so you never run out of crucial ingredients.
- Offer to help a skilled friend. Scrub vegetables and whip egg whites for them while you watch and learn.
- Make a list of 'Things I want to be able to make myself' and work up to them gradually.
- Make out a list of your own rock bottom six easy meals – baked potatoes, omelettes or scrambled eggs, pasta, grilled fish, cheese and salad, stir-fried vegetables – and cook one a night. The seventh night you eat at your mother's, cadge a meal from a friend who loves to cook or go to a restaurant.
- Simplify. Don't peel potatoes. Use cookware that can be taken to the table.
- Save yourself work and save energy by doubling or even tripling recipes.
- Ensure that you always have a supply of things you don't need to cook: fruit, vegetable sticks, yoghurt, cheese, good bread.
- Eat with the children – a light early supper is better for health and your waistline.
- Eat after the children have gone to bed – to remind yourself of what civilised dining at home is all about.

>Wild Foods

Learn the names – grab a field guide or a botanically minded friend and find out what plants are edible. Make a salad with some wild greens – delicious, nutritious and a touch of healthy survivalism. Many common plants (aka weeds) that grow in cities are edible – some are sold in gourmet food shops at a high price – amongst them lamb's quarters, purslane and dandelions. Pick your gourmet greens away from traffic and from areas where dogs roam.

Older neighbours may be able to guide you in mushroom foraging or berry picking, and you can make elderflower cordial, sloe and damson gins.

(2)

Body Care

'Body care' means the multitude of ways we soothe, smooth and decorate our bodies. The foundation of caring for our bodies is to eat well, exercise and make other positive lifestyle choices. But for most people, caring for ourselves is also about presenting ourselves to the world, in ways from hairstyles to body piercing, and about pleasurable, stress-relieving treatments.

The Meaning of Adornment

'Body adornment' is the anthropologists' term for the human desire to alter, decorate and individualise the body and appearance. Every culture has standards of beauty and particular ways of differentiating members of a society through dress and other forms of adornment. The way we decorate ourselves is a language, a form of self-expression and also of group identification. The practical purposes of adornment are to identify us – the way we look can tell others about our wealth or status, and even about our beliefs.

While some environmentalists don't think adornment is a topic worthy of serious attention, I think it's an important aspect of how we express and identify ourselves. This is not a part of life that has huge impact on the external environment, at least compared with driving or heating your flat, but it's one that has created global industries with some very particular kinds of impact: animal testing and exposure to a wide array of human-made chemicals that can cause allergic reactions, for example.

The growing market for 'natural' cosmetics doesn't necessarily eliminate the problems associated with the beauty business. Excessive packaging, advertising promises that don't pan out and an emphasis on endlessly changing fashion don't help create a sustainable world.

Scientific or Holistic?

There are two approaches to body care: the scientific and the holistic. The scientific approach is matter of fact and empirical research, based on the belief that everything can be known and studied. On the whole, it provides useful information and when it comes to something critical – like what makes an effective sun block – I'll go with the scientific approach every time.

But science can be reductive and mechanistic. A holistic approach to body care starts from a different basis: it assumes that being in tune with the forces of nature will create better products. This approach accepts that some things cannot be fully understood or analysed, and believes that natural *is* better and that intuition counts. In holistic body-care systems, natural and organic ingredients are best because they are in harmony with our skin and hair. The premise is that our skin will respond more positively to these products, that the sum is more than the individual parts. A holistic approach can seem weird, but there are some holistic products that I think are fabulous. I'm not talking about the shampoo at the supermarket that claims to be natural, but some of the artisan products made by people who believe in what they're doing.

Body care is about pleasure and self-definition, as well as about cleanliness and health. Not everything can be tested or measured in a lab. In body care, as in eating, your satisfaction is a fundamental part of the experience and your feelings about your body and how you care for it will be reflected in how you look. There's definitely room for individual choice and both approaches have something to offer as we look at body care and the environment.

Animal Testing

Most environmentalists are not radical animal rights activists. There are many organic farmers who raise animals for food and the more self-sufficient consider extreme animal rights activists to be city-bred sissies who don't understand the rough realities of rural life. Few people openly argue that it's reasonable to test cosmetics on animals, however, and there has been a recent ban on such research in Britain. The alternative testing methods are not, however, fully developed, and animals are still used to test cosmetics and other beauty products in many parts of the world, as well as for medical research.

There has been confusion about whether it's ethical to use a product that contains something that was once tested on animals. But to boycott such a product would be the equivalent of not using sugar because slavery was used on sugar plantations in the eighteenth and nineteenth centuries.

Medical experimentation is another matter. Most people take advantage of everything the medical system offers if stricken with a deadly disease. But here too alternative testing methods are being used and there is increased emphasis on the humane treatment of animals, thanks to consumer pressure.

Living Lightly

Personal and beauty products now have ingredients listings, but I'm dismayed that they are allowed to use the word 'aqua' for water. Look on products in your bathroom: how many list 'aqua' as the first ingredient? Because transporting goods is a source of much pollution – *and* contributes to global warming – moving water around the globe is a serious problem. The best thing companies could do for the environment would be to sell concentrated products for us to mix with water at home. But they worry that we wouldn't pay £3 for a bottle of skin toner if all we could see was the teaspoonful of ingredients left after the water was removed. Also, some products obviously need to be mixed and emulsified before being bottled.

As for bottles, the environmental advantage of plastic is that it is light, which means less transport impact. But plastics can leach chemicals which you don't want to drink or put on your skin. Ideally, we'd be able to refill our own glass or reused plastic bottles in a local shop. Some health shops do have shampoo and cleansers in bulk so you can bring your own container.

Q 'Wild-harvested' is a popular adjective in body care products and some foods, and it sounds good: pure nature. But the wild harvesting of plants (as well as, of course, ocean fish) threatens them with extinction.

TIPS: FOR LIVING LIGHTLY

* Buy lightweight and concentrated products.
* Choose large sizes and products that are simply packaged.
* Stock up on products you like. Buy two or three at a time, or a large bottle or package.
* Buy refills when available.
* Make your own (I put clean tap water into a spray bottle and add a few drops of lavender oil to make a delightful summer face freshener to keep in my handbag).
* Carry handkerchiefs – large men's cotton ones. They are enormously useful – much nicer to dab your face with than bits of loo paper and great for mopping up small children. They can be rinsed out and dry quickly, and you can cool off by twisting a wet handkerchief and tying it round your neck.
* Do not drop Q-tips or anything other than loo paper or flushable tampons into the toilet.

Moisturisers and Skin-care Systems

Skin-care experts say we overuse moisturisers. They're supposed to keep moisture in and protect our skin from environmental pollution. But skin has its own ways of doing both those things. Don't think you have to wear a moisturiser, especially if you have oily skin. Your goal should be to have happy skin and hair that to a large extent look after themselves.

Only you can tell what works best for you. There are skin-care lines that contain only natural ingredients, such as pure vegetable oils and genuine plant fragrances. But natural is not always more effective. Vegetable oils, for example, are more readily absorbed by the skin than mineral oils, but this means they can clog pores. Plant extracts can cause allergic reactions. If you can afford natural, organic products and you like them, go right ahead. But if your budget is modest, you shouldn't feel guilty about using basic inexpensive products, natural or not. Beauty products have relatively little environmental impact and it's better to focus your eco-conscience on other areas.

What all of us need to get used to is wearing sun screen. Most sun-screen ingredients are not natural, but they are important because the thinning of the ozone layer allows more dangerous ultraviolet (UV) radiation to reach us. The rate of malignant melanoma, a fatal skin cancer, is especially high in England, Wales and Ireland. Many Britons have fair, sun-sensitive skin and even those with darker skins need sun protection.

Smoking is the only thing that ages skin more than excessive tanning, but if you can't resist the temptation to tan, at least moderate your goal to a pleasant golden shade and give your skin plenty of time to achieve it. In addition, you should use a sun screen containing titanium dioxide, zinc oxide or avobenzone as an active ingredient to protect you against UV rays. In adverts for sun beds, the longer UV rays have been advertised as safe 'tanning' rays because they develop melanin particles in the skin and create a tan without burning. But recent research shows that UV rays are far more damaging in the long run, because they cause skin cancer and premature and irreversible ageing of the skin.

TIPS: FOR SKIN CARE AND PROTECTION

- Make a luxury pot of skin cream last for many months by applying it judiciously.
- Use vegetable- rather than petroleum-based products when possible. A jar of vegetable-based 'jelly', made for babies and available in wholefood shops, is almost identical to expensive lip salves.
- Protecting your skin from the sun should be your top priority.
- Wear a moisturiser with sun block in it *every day*, all year round. As much as 80 per cent of the sun's radiation makes it through the clouds. Make sure the sun protection factor (SPF) is at least 15 *and* the sun screen contains titanium dioxide, zinc oxide or avobenzone. A high SPF only is not enough protection.
- Shop around if your skin reacts badly to PABA, a common sun-block ingredient. There are excellent products that don't bother sensitive skin.
- All creams need to be reapplied frequently if you are swimming or sweating.
- Supplement your use of sun-screen lotion with hats, beach umbrellas and a silk wrap over your shoulders. (Be aware, however, that you can get sunburn through sheer clothing and from light reflected off pavements and water.)
- If you want a moderate but traditional tan, use self-tan lotion, coupled with a little real sunshine. No one knows for certain whether there are any long-term health risks associated with these products, though, so, as with any chemical application, be cautious.
- Consider wearing sunglasses if you are in the sun a great deal, to avoid eye problems later in life. Make sure the lenses absorb 100 per cent of both UVA and UVB light.
- Examine yourself for skin growths, itchy patches, sores that won't heal, any changes in moles or coloured areas. These could be cancerous. Skin cancer can almost always be treated successfully if caught early.

>The Ozone Layer

The ozone layer is a light filter for the Earth, protecting us from UV radiation. It is damaged by chemical gases used in various industrial processes and consumer products. Some of these gases also contribute to global warming, but the two problems are distinct: we *want* the ozone layer, but do *not* want the layer of gases creating the 'greenhouse effect'. Because the ozone layer is thinner than it should be, excessive radiation gets through to the Earth and causes skin cancer, cataracts and crop damage. Fortunately, the damage is slowly being reversed. Ozone is, ironically, a pollutant at ground level.

Cosmetics

More and more cosmetic houses are becoming aware of skin sensitivities and are cutting out irritating ingredients, particularly scents. Some standard ingredients in lipsticks have been shown to cause cancer in animals (PVP plastic, saccharin, mineral oil and artificial colours). Choose unscented products which have not been tested on animals, and avoid artificial fragrances and colours. Also avoid cosmetics containing possible hormone-disrupting chemicals: nonoxynol, octoxynol and nonylphenol ethoxylate.

Over-packaging is a problem with most cosmetics. The amount you buy is small, the price large, and the packaging makes the exchange seem less unreasonable. A few firms sell refills, which are a good idea, but on the whole there is little you can do here except buy the largest size possible and complain to the head office of your favourite firm.

 Global industry has introduced more than 70,000 synthetic chemicals into the environment in the last century, most of them since 1950.

Shower and Bath Products

Showers are more ecological than baths, as they use far less water, are less drying and you can also fit a low-flow showerhead. If you suffer from very dry skin, sponge baths are a pleasant and fast way to stay fresh between showers. None the less, a soothing bath will wash away stress and help you sleep.

Most bath mixtures are unnecessarily complicated and expensive. Bubble baths are fun, but will dry out your skin. A shampoo or even eco-friendly dish-washing liquid will create fine bubbles. Plain Epsom salts make a great mineral bath, especially with the addition of a couple of drops of essential oil. Try filling a beautiful glass jar from the antiques market for an elegant effect.

Bicarbonate of soda is a good water softener and some people find oatmeal or powdered milk in a muslin bag good for a soothing bath. For dry skin, the best treatment is a few teaspoons of vegetable oil (though any bath will dry your skin). Sea salt and fragrances can be irritating to skin, so if you're very sensitive try an unscented bath accompanied by an aromatherapy candle or lamp *(see below)*.

A bathroom can be part of an ecological home, with insulated tubs and solar water heaters to reduce energy consumption, biodegradable soaps and shampoo, and a system for using bath water in the garden.

>Soaps

Buy good-quality, unscented or naturally scented soaps. Look for handmade soaps made with natural ingredients. If you store scented soap with your shirts or underwear for a couple of months, the bars will last longer (having dried out) and your clothes will smell wonderful.

>Body Powder

Avoid powders containing talc, which can be contaminated with asbestos fibre. Talc has been associated with various forms of female reproductive cancer. Ordinary cornflour and arrowroot are soft and absorbent, and you can buy powders made from colloidal oatmeal and even silk powder!

>Anti-perspirants and Deodorants

There are two types of body-odour control: anti-perspirants, which block pores and perspiration; and deodorants, which contain something to stop the growth of the bacteria which cause odour. Both generally contain fragrance to cover up any odour as well.

Anti-perspirants generally contain aluminium chlorhydrate as their active ingredient and can contain other heavy metals. Blocking sweat glands is a bad idea and concern over the biological effects of aluminium suggest that aluminium salts should not be applied to the skin on a regular basis.

Sweating is a health function and women's growing interest in being physically active is beginning to change the dainty no-pores ideal of the past. Try limiting anti-perspirant use to times when you wear very delicate or fitted clothing. For ecological body-odour control, use pump-action or roll-on deodorants. New commercial products use natural bactericides and odour reducers: coriander, lichens, lemon and tea tree oil. Minerals are also effective. You can buy a deodorant crystal or use bicarbonate of soda – the cheapest and most effective of anything I've tried. Keep some in a pretty jar and apply gently with dampened fingertips.

Some activists believe there is an association between modern chemical anti-perspirants and breast cancer, citing the fact that many cancers occur near the armpit area. You can find varied information about this theory on the Web, should you be particularly concerned about breast cancer.

>Toothpaste and Mouthwash

Natural toothpastes, available at wholefood shops, do not contain the ammonia, ethanol, artificial flavours and colours, formaldehyde, mineral oil, saccharin, sugar or plastic compounds found in commercial brands. But dental experts say toothpaste of any kind isn't essential and the single best cleaner for teeth is bicarbonate of soda. This might not taste great, but is so good for teeth and gums that it's worth forcing yourself to try it once a week.

Fluoridated toothpaste is unnecessary for adults. If you want your children to have fluoride, give fluoride drops or tablets rather than rely on haphazard intake from toothpaste (unless your water is fluoridated, of course).

A persistent problem with bad breath is likely to be a sign of health or dental problems. Mouthwashes are not the answer, as they contain some of the same germ killers which go into bathroom disinfectants. Good oral hygiene – frequent brushing and the use of dental floss – and a healthy diet low in sugary food will do more for your teeth and breath than harsh chemical products.

>Shaving

Everyone, everywhere, alters their hair. Hair length and style have typically been an important way to tell men and women apart. That's changing, but hair removal continues to be an almost exclusively female activity. Anthropologists see it as a way for humans to assert their separateness from animals.

Before shaving, you can smooth your skin with hair conditioner or body wash, but more important is plain water – simply wet your face or legs and wait a couple of minutes before you start shaving. Try a standard razor with replaceable blades for a particularly clean shave rather than an electric razor or plastic disposable. An old-fashioned straight razor would be even better, ecologically!

Hair Care

>Shampoos

The main thing here is to buy an uncomplicated shampoo. No shampoo can perform miracles and you do want a product that won't completely strip your hair of natural oils.

One third of the shampoos sold in the UK are medicated, which means that many people think they have dandruff when they in fact don't. Once you start using an anti-dandruff shampoo, it can be difficult to stop and products you use to fight dandruff may even aggravate the problem. If you have a dandruff problem, the first things to look at are your general health and stress level. Thorough brushing and regular scalp massage can help. Your diet may be deficient in the right fats: eat more raw nuts and switch to cold-pressed safflower and virgin olive oil.

Anti-dandruff shampoos contain highly toxic chemicals, primarily selenium sulphide, which can, if swallowed, cause the degeneration of internal organs. Another dangerous chemical is recorcinol, which is easily absorbed through the skin. A seaweed-based shampoo has proved a successful treatment for some people with dandruff and tea tree oil shampoo is also recommended.

TIPS: FOR DRYING HAIR

- Electric hairdryers emit strong electromagnetic fields because they use a lot of energy. They can also damage hair. Your body, your hair and the planet will be healthier if you have a cut that is quick to dry or can dry naturally.
- If you do use an electric hairdryer, don't use it when your hair's still soaking. Towel and then air dry for a little while and use the dryer for final styling.
- The dryer will work more efficiently if you clean the intake vents every month (I use an old toothbrush).

>Hairspray

Hairsprays often contain toxic resins and propellant gases. Finely dispersed in an aerosol, they can cause a lung disease called thesaurosis. They don't do much for your skin or your eyes. Try using a safe commercial gel or pump spray.

>Hair Colouring

Many commercial hair dyes contain chemicals that are known to cause birth defects and are suspected of causing cancer. Because they can be absorbed by the scalp, consumer advocates advise against their use by pregnant women.

If you do want to colour your hair, there are a variety of safe plant-based products on the market – ask your hairdresser about them. You can also try homemade mixtures, ranging from lemon juice and camomile to lighten blond hair to black coffee or walnut hulls to cover grey in dark hair. If you must use chemical dyes, have highlights to avoid contact with your scalp.

Sticking with your natural hair colour will save considerable amounts of time and money. You'll get a better return if you invest in an excellent cut and work on having healthy, shiny hair.

Nail Care

Excessive attention to nails is one of the things that keeps women from being physically active. There's nothing wrong with wanting your hands to look pretty, but if that stops you doing things and enjoying life, something's wrong.

Try alternatives to nail varnish. Nail varnishes contain formaldehyde resin and any beauty book will tell you that nails need to be left unvarnished from time to time to 'breathe'. The acetone solvent in nail varnish not only has a strong and pervasive odour, but can cause skin rashes, dry out nails and dissolve plastics. If you use varnish, ensure that the room you are in is well-ventilated and cap the bottle of remover. Alternatively, nail buffing kits will give you an attractive natural shine with no chemicals to worry about.

A good diet will result in strong, healthy nails, so you won't need chemical nail strengtheners, which really are to be avoided – they contain drying and toxic ingredients such as formaldehyde and toluene (which is banned in California because of serious health risks).

Wearing sun screen on your hands, keeping your skin and cuticles moisturised, and wearing rubber gloves when doing housework will also help keep your nails in good shape. Active and competent hands (neatly groomed) are the female hands of the future.

Eye Care

Glasses are more eco-friendly than contact lenses because they require no solutions, tablets and sterilisation. But that's not going to persuade many people to go back to them. If you wear contacts, ask for lenses and a lens care system that are as simple as possible. Manufacturers make tons of money on the daily solution tubes and tiny bottles. The cheapest safe system will be easiest on the environment, and a good professional will be honest with you about what you really need. Plain saline solution, for example, makes perfect eye drops, and my practitioner told me I could boil and then refill sample bottles for travel.

Eyes, like teeth, have regenerative capacity. In Germany, there are state-funded courses to train Bates eye therapy teachers and you can contact one in Britain *(see Resources)*.

Body Piercing and Tattooing

Both of these popular practices go back to ancient times. Along with scarification, they are basic forms of body modification practised by men and women all over the world. They can be seen as a statement of group or personal identification. Unlike other forms of body adornment, they are permanent. It remains difficult and often impossible to remove tattoos.

Both practices involve breaking the skin, which breaches the body's protective barriers. It's always important to ensure that the person who does the work is experienced, professional and scrupulous about hygiene to avoid the risk of infection. Hepatitis B has been transmitted through tattooing and tetanus and HIV may be a risk. Piercing of the mouth is especially painful and potentially hazardous, because it allows an extra point of entry – direct to the bloodstream – of any food toxin you might eat.

Like any other medical procedure, the needles used in piercing and tattooing become biohazard waste, which is difficult and expensive to handle, and other waste includes latex gloves and disposable instruments.

Body Treatments

This isn't the place to cover treatments at length, but the simplest and most universal body treatment, massage, deserves a mention. Massage needs no equipment and anyone can learn to do it. It relieves stress, compensates for some of the ways we misuse our bodies and is companionable – an ideal part of eco living.

A professional massage can be wonderful, but for lifelong benefits it makes sense to learn the basic techniques yourself – and encourage a friend or partner to learn too. There are numerous good books about massage, as well as classes and videos. Special oils aren't necessary, but you'll want some kind of oil or lotion that isn't absorbed too quickly. The idea is to provide some slip against the skin.

While a massage table is nice, people have managed for thousands of years with the floor or a firm bed or a sturdy table. In fact, it's possible to have a pleasant massage while sitting in a chair. Some companies even allow massage therapists to come into the office and offer 15-minute chair massages to employees.

>Aromatherapy

Aromatherapy is the use of essential oils extracted from a wide array of plant materials to enhance physiological and psychological health. There are dozens, perhaps hundreds, of essential oils to choose from. Lavender is perhaps the most versatile of oils; it is well known for its calming effect and is also used as an antiseptic. Peppermint, which contains menthol, is considered an intellectual stimulant. Whether you believe this or not – aromatherapy is popular but not proven – no one can deny that stimulating our noses with delicious fragrances is deeply pleasurable.

Essential oil means that the oil is the essence of the plant, a concentrated fragrance. It's economical to buy small bottles of oils you love (as well as lavender and peppermint, lemon is another basic, but I happen to adore geranium) to add to a vegetable oil of your choice, to a bath, lotions or oil lamps. If you have sensitive skin, it's best not to use essential oils or other fragrances directly on it, as fragrances are the most common source of skin reactions. If your skin isn't sensitive, you can rub a little essential oil on pulse points as a scent.

Look for oils from organically grown plants. The best source I know of is Neal's Yard in London *(see Resources)*. Read the labels: many 'aromatherapy' oils have been diluted with vegetable oil, which makes them poor value.

Sanitary Protection

While modern sanitary products have made life easier, there are health and environmental issues related to one-use only tampons and sanitary towels. There are also some eco alternatives you should know about.

Tampons can cause a potential fatal illness, toxic shock syndrome. The Women's Environmental Network has worked to raise women's awareness about the use of pesticides on cotton, and the use of rayon and cotton that can contain traces of dioxins, a highly dangerous poison. Another problem is that a high percentage of sewage is simply dumped into the sea, and the plastic applicator tubes for tampons and the plastic liners in sanitary pads create permanent beach litter and endanger sea animals.

Alternatives include rubber cups, similar to a diaphram, that need to be changed less frequently than tampons. These are great for sportswomen. Some women use, and reuse, natural sponges. You can buy washable menstrual pads made from organic, unbleached and sometimes brightly patterned cottons *(contact the Women's Environmental Network for sources)*.

TIPS: FOR SANITARY PROTECTION
- Never flush sanitary pads or any plastic.
- Consider using a non-disposable system of sanitary protection. The modern products are a far cry from the simple rags our great great grandmothers had to use!
- Avoid tampons containing ultra-absorbent materials which increase the growth rate of the bacteria which cause toxic shock syndrome.
- Choose tampons made from biodegradable cardboard and unbleached cotton.
- Look for organic cotton tampons in wholefood shops (unfortunately they're quite expensive – but prices are coming down).

Sleeping

Although in most ways our world is speeding up and more and more people say they are sleep deprived, we aren't sleeping any less. However, we aren't getting the rest we need and instead of waking up invigorated too many of us are dragging ourselves out of bed. This may reflect unexplored psychological and social aspects of our hectic modern way of life.

Q Bedding is now available that is made from untreated or organic cotton. Different colours of cotton are grown, so organic, undyed bed linens come in ecru, pale green, or light tan. Linen is expensive, but will outlast cotton sheets by 10 years or more. Hemp sheets *(see Chapter 4)* last nearly for ever.

TIPS: FOR GOOD SLEEP

- Have some quiet reflective time before trying to get to sleep. Plan the next day so you don't jump out of bed feeling frantic.
- Stretching and gentle exercise will help you sleep soundly, but don't do physical jerks just before bed. (Exercise can also wake you up. Try a walk or run in the late afternoon if you want to be alert for the evening.)
- Alcohol may put you to sleep, but it doesn't promote healthy sleep. Try traditional warm milk or camomile tea instead.
- Avoid falling asleep in front of the TV; new studies show that for children in particular, evening television watching interferes with the transition to sleep.
- Create an environment conducive to sleep. It should be quiet and dark. Minimise the electrical equipment in your bedroom, especially near your bed. Some people find certain smells soothing and there are herbal pillows containing ingredients like dried hops (a soporific) to encourage sleep.
- Waking up naturally is another way to promote physical and psychological health: our abrupt rising to strident alarms may also be affecting how we sleep. Try orienting your room to the east, if you can, and encourage yourself to wake at a certain time, before the alarm goes off (set the alarm, as backup). A light alarm, that provides gradual brightening, is also an option. Ten or fifteen minutes of peaceful re-acclimatising to the waking world will make every day go better.

What You Wear

I love clothes. I envy the elegant way French and Italian women wear their clothes, and admire the vibrant traditional clothing worn by African women and men. Dressing is a necessity but it's also an important form of human adornment and group identity – and a big business, too.

The clothes we choose to wear affect the environment and the lives of garment workers all over the world. Even jewellery has ecological consequences. Mining is a polluting business, which means that diamonds from the ocean floor and gold from the Australian outback come with high eco pricetags. The good news is that the fashion industry is often alert to issues and new designers are coming up with clothes that are good for us *and* good for the planet.

It's a shame that few of us make our own clothes – we've lost a whole range of personal expression, creativity and skill. Dressmaking, knitting and embroidery can be as satisfying as cooking, though they are more difficult to pick up. Ask someone to teach you so you can make clothes with new wool and beautiful fabrics or, even better, with vintage materials from the market.

Social Issues

When we buy foreign-made goods we may be encouraging sweatshops run by huge international companies, where people are paid 50p for making a £60 pair of trainers. Children in developing countries like Pakistan are a major source of labour for companies based in Europe and North America. Working conditions are sometimes hazardous to their health, as they ingest harsh chemicals and breathe massive amounts of dust. Toys and carpets are also made by children.

Although governments try to step in and mandate better controls, there is just not enough money in these countries to maintain proper supervision. We, as consumers, are the most powerful agent against child labour. We can make a difference by boycotting the products of any company that supports the use of child labour and buying from the organisations and companies are making an effort to provide people in developing nations with real trade opportunities. *Visit http://www.sweatshops.org for more information.*

New to You

Buying things secondhand is a way to save money as you recycle. For household items, there are auctions, sale rooms and boot fairs, ranging from the seedy to the exalted. My best 'finds' come from jumble sales packed with women intent on bargains, the best such sales being at churches and schools in prosperous areas. Charity shops exist to raise money, so prices are higher than at a jumble sale. Resale and 'vintage' clothing shops are more expensive still, but the quality is also higher again.

Fabrics

New fabrics are being developed all the time, sometimes for beauty and sometimes for practical reasons. High-tech fabrics for outdoor wear aren't necessary, but they can make it far easier to stay warm and dry, while breathable waterproof gear will make it more comfortable to walk or cycle.

The greatest environmental impact comes from our treating clothing as disposable and from chemicals used in their manufacture, so the most important consideration is whether you're buying a garment that you'll be able to wear a lot and keep for a long time, not whether it's made of natural fibre. Choose versatile garments that you really like and will want to keep and you'll help the planet. Beyond that, however, there are important fabric choices, outlined below.

>Natural and Organic Cotton

Even cotton can be loaded with dyes, pesticide residues from growing and chemical residues from processing, and 'no-iron' fabrics are treated with formaldehyde resin.

Organic cotton is grown without chemicals and does not contain finishing agents like formaldehyde. It is grown in many colours: shades of green, brown and even terracotta. The colours of natural cotton deepen after washing. Checked and herringbone fabrics are woven without any dyes at all!

An industry representative says that although untreated 'natural' cotton is more expensive because it requires special handling and equipment, once production is undertaken on a larger scale, manufacturers will save money on dyes, making it less expensive.

One of the growing trends in the bed and bath retail market is unbleached, undyed and untreated cotton sheets and towels. These creamy coloured items are softer and more comfortable, as well as better for the environment.

>Eco-fleece

Eco-fleece is made from plastic drinks bottles – 90 per cent post-consumer content. Not a bad idea, but plastic bottles weren't designed to be worn next to your skin and they will never biodegrade.

Similarly, blends of eco-fleece with cotton or wool, in spite of the green labelling (recycled and organic), are neither biodegradable nor recyclable. Avoid these fabrics and stick with pure eco-fleece or 100 per cent natural material.

>Tencel

Tencel fabric is made from the cellulose of trees that are grown on managed tree farms on land that is not suitable for food crops or grazing. The process used to extract the cellulose is non-toxic and free of chemicals.

Tencel can be found in fabrics that resemble denim as well as soft cottons. It is an easy-care fabric.

>Hemp

Hemp comes from the stem of the Cannabis sativa plant and is so durable that it was used in ancient times to make sails. It was also the original material for Levi jeans.

The use of hemp has increased in recent years, due to its eco-friendly features. It has a much higher yield per acre than cotton, requires far less water and doesn't need pesticides, herbicides or chemical fertilisers.

Hemp is much like linen in its breathability and comfort.

>Organic Wool

Wool is good – it is a versatile, warm fabric that is naturally fire retardant and soil and stain resistant. Organic wool is even better, as it is not chemically treated and is generally dyed with low-impact dyes.

Look on the Web for green clothing companies like Green Fibres (www.greenfibres.com). More options are being made available all the time and we need to support innovative designers and new green materials.

>Organic Buttons

Some buttons are now made of corozo and tagua nuts from the rainforests of South America. They look like bone. Any button made from biodegradable material – wood or shell – is probably preferable to plastic. I save favourite antique buttons and sew them onto new sweaters and jackets

❶ Dyes are among the most polluting aspects of the fashion industry. Vegetable dyes have softer colours and tend to fade, but some small manufacturers are using low-impact biodegradable dyes. Choosing fabrics in natural colours will help.

Tread Lightly: Shoes

At the moment, the most ecological shoe is made entirely of leather, because it will biodegrade. Shoe leather, however, is treated with chemicals. Most modern shoes have longer-wearing and more comfortable synthetic rubber soles, but with each step, they release particles which may contaminate soil and add another burden to the environment.

Shoes should be made from material that will nourish the soil instead of harming it. Low-impact dyed leather is the best choice (or take a look at vegetarian shoes – www.vegetarian-shoes.co.uk), but more practically you should buy as few pairs of shoes as possible and wear them out. Leather, by the way, has a quality that none of the top 'new' materials have: it ages gracefully and can look good for years.

Clothes Care

You can look after your clothes in a number of ways that are better for the fabrics and indeed also for our health as well as for the environment. The following section will give you some ideas to think about.

>Washing

Modern washing powders are detergents, with a variety of additives including optical brighteners, enzymes and fragrances. Biodegradable, enzyme-free alternatives are available from various mail order and retail suppliers. They may need the addition of a water softener, however, to get clothes clean in hard water. Before you switch to a washing powder which does not contain optical brighteners, it may help to run your clothes through a wash cycle with a double dose of softener.

Green catalogues often sell ceramic disks or balls that are supposed to replace washing powder in your machine. When first marketed, they were supposed to be used alone, but now additional bleaching agent is recommended. A *Which?* test found that plain water worked as well (and it does, for clothes that aren't really dirty). I stick with a basic unscented eco-friendly detergent and use as little as possible.

When you wash silk and wool by hand, use a mild non-alkaline soap such as Ecover Wool Wash.

>Stain Removal

- Start with cold water, particularly on protein-based spots like blood, egg or gravy. Hot water will cook and set the stain.
- Plain soda water works on many stains.
- Pouring salt on a wine stain is usually effective and is worth trying on fruit and beetroot stains.
- A borax solution can be successful – one part borax to eight parts water – for blood, chocolate, coffee and tea, mildew, mud and urine.
- Plain old boiling water is good for fruit and tea stains – preferably poured on taut fabric from a great height.

- Glycerine from the chemist gets grass stains out of cricket trousers.

>Moth Protection

Mothballs are made of paradichlorobenzene, a volatile chemical which is a respiratory irritant and can cause depression, seizures and long-term damage to the kidneys and liver. Cedarwood, lavender and natural camphor are natural traditional moth repellants, but the most important thing is to ensure that woollens are cleaned before being stored. Pressing with a steam iron or tumbledrying will also kill any moth eggs.

Many natural products are recommended for protection from moths, from orange peel to lavender flowers to bay leaves. Cedar chips or a cedar chest are said to discourage moths. Freezing will kill moths and their eggs, so I occasionally put my favourite jumpers in the freezer for a day.

>Whiteners

Use an oxygen-based bleach, if necessary. Sunshine will bleach white clothes (beware, hot sun can fade colours quickly). An old method was to spread whites on green vegetation – a lawn, for example – as the oxygen produced by the plants is said to be helpful. Now and then I'm very old fashioned and boil my tea towels and dishcloths.

>Fabric Conditioners

People often use softeners to make clothes smell 'fresh', but hanging them outside does a far better job and you don't have to worry about possible allergic reactions.

Try putting herbal bags in your drawers and closets.

>Dry Cleaning

'Dry' cleaning uses a solvent instead of water to wash clothes. Carbon tetrachloride was used until recently but has been found to cause cancer. The dry-cleaning industry has a history of fatal worker illness. The most common solvents at the moment are two organochlorines, trichlorotrifluoroethane and perchloroethylene. They are both toxic and the former is a chlorofluorohydrocarbon, one of the CFCs which are causing the deterioration of the ozone layer. Short-term acute exposure to these solvents can cause giddiness, nausea and unconsciousness. Chronic exposure is even worse, because the compounds accumulate in body tissue and lead to organ damage and cancer risk. Prolonged exposure to perchloroethylene can cause breast and liver cancer.

Although dry-cleaning chemicals evaporate after a short time, the environmental consequences of manufacturing, transporting and disposing of them mean that we should avoid dry cleaning as much as possible. The best advice is not to buy clothes that are difficult or hazardous to clean. Some garments labelled 'Dry clean only' can be washed by hand or even machine (manufacturers sometimes use these labels as a precautionary measure) and some designers are seriously working on clothes that are easier to care for.

Clothes that do require special treatment are tailored clothes with many layers of different fabrics in lining and interlining.

If you do have clothes dry cleaned, ensure that they are thoroughly aired, either outdoors or in an unoccupied room, before being put away.

The US Environmental Protection Agency has been studying 'wet cleaning' in an effort to reduce exposure to hazardous dry-cleaning chemicals. The benefits of this new process are that it doesn't require solvents, the initial investment to get a shop going is less than that for dry cleaning and consumers prefer wet-cleaned clothes because they smell better.

In the meantime, there are several ways in which dry cleaners can help protect the environment as well as lower their costs. Recommend that your dry cleaner:

- recycles hangers
- reuses plastic garment bags
- uses less cleaning solvent
- becomes a donation drop-off site for a local charity

TIPS: FOR CLOTHES CARE

Equip your Laundry
Include:
- a clothes drying rack
- solid shaped hangers
- a shoe rack or bag and shoetrees (or tissue)
- a clothes brush and lint remover or tape
- a mending kit
- an ironing board and iron; sprinkler

Make Clothes Last Longer
- Air clothes before putting them away.
- Brush wool jackets thoroughly after every wearing with strong sweeping strokes, first against the nap and then with the nap.
- Let garments and shoes rest between wearings.

Ironing
- Don't iron if you don't have to. If you use a tumbledryer, fold clothes quickly, smoothing and stretching the fabric, and you won't need to iron. Some fabrics drip-dry beautifully, or you can cultivate an elegantly rumpled look. Linen itself can be smoothed when damp (shape the collar with your fingers), so no ironing is required.
- If you use a dryer, simply smooth clothes while they're warm to eliminate ironing.
- Iron in large batches at a time to save on electricity and use a heat-reflective cover.
- Do not machine dry or iron fabrics bone dry. Stop when they are almost dry.
- Get a crisp finish by using traditional powdered starch from the chemist.

Eco Living

Energy Saving

- Wash full loads, and keep the cycles as short and cool as possible. Clothes can be rinsed in cold water, but a hot wash is preferable to using large amounts of detergent. Let the machine fill with hot water heated by your gas system, rather than allowing it to heat electrically in the machine.
- Use a front-loading washing machine; they use less water and energy than toploaders.
- Run automatic dryer loads back to back, while the dryer drum is hot.
- Hang clothes outside to dry or on racks indoors; if necessary finish in the airing cupboard. I have a small rack, which is very convenient, right above my washing machine, and another rack in a nearby room.
- A spin dryer can halve the time and energy needed to tumbledry a load of clothes, even after they have been spun in a washing machine. It makes drying clothes on racks much faster too.
- Use the local launderette or share a laundry with friends or neighbours.

Staying Well (4)

Health is not only about the way we care for ourselves, but also about how we care for one other, the health of the society we create together. Good health means having the physical and psychological resources to respond to the demands of your life and environment.

Today, along with continuing debate over health-care provision, medical malpractice and the modern insistence on medical solutions to all life's problems, there's a promising resurgence of the concept of holistic health, an approach that: (1) recognises that individual health depends on a variety of environmental, social and economic factors; (2) sees adequate health care as a basic human right.

Physically, we are hunter-gatherers and the rapid technological changes of the past century have put our bodies in a vulnerable position because we have not adapted to the modern environment. Our lives are sheltered in a way which our ancestors would not have been able to imagine. Fewer children die in infancy as a result, but as we grow up we lose out through becoming alienated from our bodies. The amount of time we spend indoors under artificial lighting, in sealed buildings, enduring long and stressful commutes, repetitive jobs, electrical wiring and appliances and traffic noise affects the way we feel. Allergies and food sensitivities are on the increase, heart disease and cancer are the so-called 'diseases of civilisation' and too many of us suffer from complaints which interfere with what we would like to do in our lives.

While the environment has always had an effect on human health, the modern world presents a multitude of new challenges, from the recurrence of tuberculosis to multiple chemical sensitivity. And our medical system itself has an impact on the global environment in many ways, from animal experimentation to genetic modification, from dangerous overuse of antibiotics to the growing amount of hazardous medical waste. This chapter focuses on the relationship between our health and the environment, and on the many positive choices we can make.

A Chemical Onslaught

Products we use every day contain chemicals which are known to be carcinogenic (cancer-causing), mutagenic (mutation-causing) and teratogenic ('monster'-causing, that is, leading to birth defects). New chemicals are being developed every day and put into use without adequate testing. Governments recognise this but consider it impossible to test everything for risk to human health or the environment, so in most countries testing is restricted to food and drugs.

Q Our bodies contain traces of some 500 chemicals that did not even exist in 1920 and global travel means that virtually everyone on the planet is exposed to viruses that in the past would stay put.

Perhaps the most serious danger posed by chemicals is 'hormone mimicking', thought to be caused by organochlorines, chlorine-based chemical compounds in wide use throughout the world in pesticides, plastics and synthetic materials. Organochlorines include DDT (traces of which are still turning up in our food), PCBs and dioxins, as well as commonly used herbicides, fungicides, germicides, preservatives and solvents.

They mimic the effects of oestrogen and accumulate in tissue, particularly in fatty tissue.

Dioxins are chemical compounds that not only cause cancer but also have subtle effects on foetal development and the human immune system, even at extremely low levels. Waste incineration and chlorine bleaching are major sources of dioxins in the environment.

Polychlorinated biphyenyls, or PCBs, are known to cause sterility and cancer. They were once heavily used in the electronics industry, where they were valued for their inertness, but in the environment their chemical stability means that they do not break down. Contaminated soil has to be removed and rivers dredged.

A growing number of people are finding themselves sensitive to food additives and colourings, chlorine bleach, pesticides, enzyme detergents and other chemical products, and people in many professions are exposed to new hazards.

In addition, chemicals can affect our genes. Some health disorders are being seen in the children and grandchildren of people exposed to particular hazards.

Pregnant women and their unborn babies are particularly vulnerable to chemical toxins. Whatever the mother consumes or comes into contact with will affect the baby. *(See Chapter 16 for more about this topic.)* Hospital operating room staff, for example, have suffered a high rate of miscarriage and infertility, resulting from exposure to anaesthetics, which has led to improvements in ventilation.

Children are also vulnerable, as they take in more air and more food in relation to their body weight than do adults, and they are more sensitive to environmental toxins, just as they are to ionising radiation. Children's reactions to chemicals can include hyperactivity and even psychiatric disorders. In the United States, new regulations to provide special protection for children are being initiated.

We add to the chemical onslaught with an excessive range of disinfectants, thereby showing a fundamental misunderstanding of the ecology of health. We don't get ill simply because there are viruses around. Bacteria, viruses, fungi and protozoa are with us all the time and we need many of them. Bacteria in our digestive tract help to digest food and organisms on our skin protect us from potentially harmful bacteria. There are, of course, a few highly dangerous bacteria to be concerned about and you'll find more about protecting yourself from them in Chapter 1 *(see pages 10–11)* and Chapter 8.

While our bodies are able to deal with a certain quantity of environmental poisons, each person's chemical tolerance point is different. Once this has been passed, severe and debilitating illness can result. It's claimed that exposure to certain chemicals, especially formaldehyde, can 'sensitise' people, damaging their immune systems so that in future they will have severe reactions to things they previously tolerated.

Possible symptoms of environmental illness include asthma and eczema, depression, chronic fatigue, skin rashes and migraine headaches. A growing speciality called clinical ecology, or environmental medicine, concentrates on the way foods and food additives, chemicals, radiation and other pollutants cause disease, allergies, depression and fatigue.

Indoor Air Pollution

We're spending more time than ever before indoors, but the air inside our houses and offices is often two to five times more polluted than the air outside! Our building materials, consumer products and personal activities all create invisible pollution known as volatile organic compounds (VOCs). VOCs are produced by particle board, soft plastics, plastic foams, caulkings, paints and varnishes, office machines, cleaners, personal products and even some foods. Air fresheners, moth crystals and aerosol sprays and solvents are particularly hazardous, while using a gas cooker or burning an aromatherapy candle can provide carbon monoxide and particulate levels as high as those in heavy traffic.

Emissions from most of these products decline rapidly after a few days or weeks, but some, such as those from new carpets and particle board, last longer. Over-exposure can result in dizziness, headaches and nausea, respiratory problems such as asthma, and weakened immune systems. This indoor air pollution causes respiratory complaints and suppresses the immune system by reducing lymphocyte and antibody production.

The most important steps you can take to improve air quality are to reduce your energy use *(see Chapters 7, 9 and 12)*, support organic farming *(see Chapter 1)* and use non-toxic DIY and cleaning supplies *(see Resources)*.

Q Improved draughtproofing can increase indoor air pollution because we are saving energy by reducing air exchange with the outside. As a result, concentrations of VOCs can build up to dangerous levels.

TIPS: FOR CLEAN BREATHING

- Spend as much time as possible outdoors, preferably in clean air spots such as mountains, beaches and some parts of the countryside.
- Use non-toxic building materials, cleaning and DIY supplies.
- Avoid all aerosols (choose pump action instead) because the fine mist lingers and is absorbed through the lungs.
- Ensure that all heating appliances are vented outside. Do not use paraffin heaters or portable gas heaters.
- Heat your house to a moderate, minimal comfort level so you can increase ventilation without wasting energy. *(See Chapter 7.)*

Q Washing at high temperatures lets chemicals into the air and we breathe them in. Dishwashers with powerful commercial washing powder create a plume of toxic vapour.

Allergies

Allergies are an over-reaction of the immune system, the body's defence mechanism, to irritating stimuli that the body generally copes with without symptoms.

Allergies are on the increase nowadays and many people believe themselves to be allergic to some food or household substance. This is not surprising when one considers the rapid increase in the number of new chemicals that have come into use in recent decades. But allergic reactions are also connected with individual immune responses and we seem to be getting more sensitive to natural substances – pollen, for example – as well. Hay fever and asthma appear to be on the rise, while cases of asthma have doubled in the last fifteen years.

Research suggests several causes for the increase in over-reaction. First, we are able to provide far more hygienic surroundings than at any time in the past and as a result babies never develop strong immune systems. Secondly, only 25 per cent of British children are breastfed for the recommended minimum of four months. Breastfeeding is an important part of the process of developing a strong immune system, as a child is able to build his own immune system with help from the mother's antibodies. Breastfed babies are substantially healthier as infants and generally healthier throughout their lives. Thirdly, the pollution in our environment and the number of man-made chemical products we are exposed to in our homes and workplaces create an extra source of stress for weakened immune systems.

The Impact of Modern Health Care

We are living longer because of generally improved living conditions and high-tech medical care, but for many people health has come to mean merely the absence of an obviously debilitating disease. Illness has become something to conquer with an instant remedy (advertisements for aspirin talk about 'hitting back at pain'), so it doesn't interfere with our busy lives. We treat the body as a machine which needs an occasional oiling and maybe a replacement part now and then, instead of as a complex and self-sustaining system.

The availability of medical attention and the demands of modern life mean that many people abdicate responsibility for their health, demanding unlimited access to medication and medical care while ignoring indignities medicine can't treat (but they themselves could prevent) like breathlessness after climbing a few flights of stairs. Even homoeopathic pills and vitamins can be taken in place of making positive life changes.

Legal prescription drugs are one of the most profitable businesses on Earth (at least 12.5 per cent of the NHS budget is spent on them) and professional kudos – and grant money – go to those who come up with expensive, resource-intensive medical 'miracles' – miracles that usually result in increased profits for pharmaceutical companies. This can lead to research that goes beyond the bounds of what is reasonable.

It's not ecologically or socially sound to try to keep everyone from dying; the Earth simply can't sustain the increasing human numbers. Instead, our emphasis should be on improving quality, not length, of life, with a progressive, ecological approach to health care that focuses on lifestyle change and the human element in maintaining health. This approach would emphasise preventative care and the links between environmental pollution and human disease. Some three-quarters of all cancers, for example, are caused by food, smoke and chemicals. The increase in certain cancers, especially in younger people, is thought by many experts to be the result of specific environmental exposures.

Q Hospitals use huge quantities of disposable products. Environmentalists in the United States have started a coalition to stop the incineration of health-care waste.

>Dangerous Antibiotics

Our connections with other people – the human disease ecosystem – can be clearly seen in the growing global problem of drug resistance caused by antibiotics being over-prescribed, over-used or improperly taken by patients. If one person doesn't take the full dose of an antibiotic, the bacteria may mutate into drug-resistant strains which then spread to other people. We also ingest antibiotics in animal products, because many livestock are routinely dosed with antibiotics because they promote fast growth. Some experts say that before long antibiotics will be useless and we'll be back to the pre-World War II situation where a bacterial infection was often deadly.

Many serious infectious diseases, long thought to be under control, have re-emerged in recent years as significant health risks. There are now mutant strains of rheumatic fever, meningitis and malaria which are resistant to known antibiotics, and hospitals have faced mini-plagues of bacteria which spread between patients. Tuberculosis (TB), the leading infectious cause of death among adults, is drug-resistant in more than half the countries of the world.

Because antibiotics disrupt the natural balance of organisms throughout our bodies, women who take antibiotics often end up with vaginal yeast infections, which can become chronic. This particular health complaint has dramatically increased – by over 50 per cent according to some reports – in the last decade.

>Medical Radiation

We receive higher doses of dangerous radiation from medical procedures than from any other source, except rare industrial accidents. While X-rays have become routine, the radiation doses given by different equipment can vary by a factor of 1,000. Medical X-rays cause some cancers, and some experts believe that X-ray radiation contributes to other health problems and genetic disorders in offspring.

If your leg has been shattered in an accident, you are unlikely to quibble about the X-rays needed to make a decision about how to set it. But be discriminating about routine exposure to radiation – it's your DNA:

- Do not agree to 'defensive' X-rays and be cautious about routine dental X-rays.
- Discuss alternative diagnosis methods.
- Ensure that you are wearing a lead shield to protect the rest of your body, especially your sex organs.
- Insist that X-ray films are transferred with you if you are referred to another doctor so you won't need new ones to provide a baseline.
- Do not have X-rays during pregnancy or while trying to conceive, unless absolutely unavoidable.
- Do not allow X-rays for children, unless it is a genuine medical emergency.

>Dentistry

An ecological approach to dental care sees healthy teeth and gums as one sign of general good health. A sound diet, with plenty of chewy foods and fibre, lots of calcium and other minerals, is important for adult teeth and even more important for children. Fill your fridge with nutritious snacks and encourage your children to eat, or drink, foods with plenty of calcium (milk and cheeses, nuts, sardines, greens).

The Department of Health is now advising dentists to leave teeth alone whenever possible and not to drill out areas of sound tooth in order to put in fillings. This reflects an awareness that teeth are not dead; they can re-mineralise and if left untouched, small patches of decay will sometimes disappear, especially with improvements in diet and brushing.

Metal amalgam fillings have attracted much attention, because dental amalgam contains up to 50 per cent mercury, a highly toxic metal. Some dentists think that slow release of this poison damages the immune system. Mercury also vaporises, presenting a hazard to dental workers. If you've had amalgam fillings for years and are in good health, it's safer to leave them in place. But next time you have a filling, ask about white bonded composite. Such fillings are tricky to do correctly, however, so you want a dentist accustomed to using this material.

The Active Patient

- Find out as much as you can about your health, including any medication you are taking. The Web is an invaluable resource, as are libraries.
- Keep a list of medications.
- Be honest about your weight, how much exercise you take and how much you drink.
- Observe and record your symptoms.
- Prepare a list of questions to take with you, and take notes.
- Be assertive. Ask 'What will happen if I wait to try this?' It's better, when possible, to let your body heal itself.
- Consult a complementary medicine practitioner if you have a chronic problem that conventional treatment doesn't seem to be able to solve.

Complementary Medicine

Orthodox medicine is beginning to accept that non-conventional complementary treatments are popular and often effective. The Health Education Authority issues a *Guide to Complementary Medicine and Therapies*, rating different approaches for medical credibility, scientific research, availability and popularity. In a recent survey, three-quarters of respondents wanted to have complementary therapies available on the NHS and some GPs now refer patients to the more accepted complementary practitioners – acupuncturists, osteopaths and hypnotherapists. With public demand for their services growing by an estimated 20 per cent each year, complementary practitioners are becoming a significant part of our health-care system.

Most of these practitioners take an holistic view of medicine. Holistic medicine aims to treat the whole person, not just a symptom. Many holistic practitioners do not like to think in terms of 'disease'. Instead, they describe a particular set of symptoms as a common pattern of coping responses. The actual cause, which is what they want to deal with, may be different for each person, as each person responds to his or her physical and social environment in a different way. So, every treatment needs to be individually tailored. This sort of analysis takes more time that a typical office visit to your doctor (or the five minutes you are booked with a hospital consultant) and a first visit is likely to take an hour or so because the practitioner will want to discuss your health history and way of life.

A significant problem with alternative health care is that there is no legal restriction on who is qualified to practise in many fields. There are, however, bodies which accredit schools and award particular qualifications, and you should consult one of these before choosing a practitioner *(see Resources)*.

Most people rely on the recommendation of friends or colleagues to find a good practitioner, but plan to shop around, just as you would for a good plumber. If you don't have much money, ask about a free introductory session or reduced fees. Going to a group practice is a good idea, because you can easily move on to someone else if the person you first consult feels that this is appropriate. A good therapist will be aware of other disciplines and of conventional medical treatment. Look for a practitioner who explains the treatment, enlists your support, is clear about the results you can expect and takes an individual approach to your health problem.

Self Care

You are your most important health-care provider and you can do more than any doctor or osteopath to improve your general state of health. Taking responsibility for your health and believing that you can take steps to deal with fatigue or stress or a lack of fitness are important aspects of eco living.

Arrange some time for a personal health assessment. It may help to simply close your eyes and mentally examine yourself from head to toe:

- What condition is your hair in, your eyes, your skin? How is your hearing? Are you overweight or underweight? What about aches and pains, creaky joints? What about athlete's foot or mouth ulcers, or even general stiffness?
- Do you feel tired all the time or get depressed easily? Do you have any feelings of anger or aggression? Allergies or hay fever? Nervous mannerisms?
- Consider your job, the place you live, your relationships, your way of life. How satisfied are you? Can you laugh at yourself?

Fatigue is a sign that your body (and maybe your mind) needs a rest. Indigestion is a request for a change of diet. A chronically stiff neck might tell you that you are tense, or that you're spending too much time hunched over your desk. Let each of these things trigger your thoughts about how you might, over time, take steps to improve your own life and the world around you.

Q The way we deal with stress has an impact on our immune systems. So, what social support networks do we have – and how willing are we to offer support to friends in need?

>The Basics of Self Care
- Don't smoke.
- Don't drink much alcohol.

- Do drink plenty of water.
- Maintain a healthy weight.
- Get plenty of exercise *(see Chapter 5 for more on this).*
- Get enough sleep, fresh air and natural light.
- Surround yourself with things and people you love.
- Reduce your exposure to pollutants at work and at home.
- Get most of your nutrients from foods, not from supplements.
- Go through the bathroom cabinet, return old drugs to the chemist and separate non-prescription drugs you'd be better off without: laxatives, antacids (often high in aluminium) and diuretics.
- Don't medicate the effects of stress. Try a nap or a short walk, or a cup of hot sage or peppermint tea.
- Become informed about health research and medical treatment.
- Be proactive when you do see a health-care professional – ask questions and get involved in your diagnosis and treatment options.

See also the information on noise (pages 158–60) and eyes (pages 155–7).

Light and Health

Human beings need light to stay healthy, in spite of the modern dangers of too much sunlight. We naturally gravitate towards light and find our mood lifting whenever the sun shines. Unfortunately, modern living isolates us from natural light – we spend almost all our time indoors, under artificial lights. And we no longer get enough vitamin D, essential for calcium absorption and strong bones, from exposure to sunlight.

Some people suffer from a condition called seasonal affective disorder (SAD) during winter months. SAD is thought to be the result of over-production of a hormone called melatonin. Its symptoms are severe depression (which lifts at the arrival of spring), accompanied by cravings for carbohydrates, weight gain and excessive sleeping. Therapy includes sitting in front of huge sets of full-spectrum lights.

A more natural approach to the 'winter blues' – which all of us can use – is to spend more time outside. Spend a minimum of 15 minutes a day outside in summer and 30 minutes in winter (when the sun is less intense).

TIPS: FOR MAKING THE MOST OF LIGHT

- Try to work close to a window (preferably open). Turn the area near a window or a narrow balcony into a sunny spot to work and eat at.
- Make a sunny part of your garden an outdoor room by equipping it with a table, comfortable seats and adequate protection from direct summer sun.
- Walk or cycle instead of driving.
- Choose outdoor activities and sports in preference to indoor ones.
- Don't wear sunglasses unnecessarily. Your eyes need some sunlight unfiltered by lenses or window panes.
- Always wear sun screen! (See Chapter 2.)

Green Sex

Sex rates high on any list of sustainable pleasures. It doesn't waste resources or create pollution and it's a free, natural, low-tech form of recreation. But it's also the only area in which an ecological viewpoint pits us against a natural process: making babies. There are more than six billion people on the planet now and over-population will be a major twenty-first-century problem. So contraception is an essential part of eco living, in spite of concerns about the health effects of both spermicides and the Pill, and about environmental issues including condom disposal and battery-operated sex aids.

Humans have tried to prevent unwanted pregnancy for thousands of years. There are many proponents of natural family planning (NFP), or the 'rhythm method', both for religious and health reasons. Modern NFP is done with a thermometer and charts and attentiveness to the woman's physical changes during ovulation. Too many people have found, however, that NFP produces a large natural family! The health risks associated with modern forms of contraception are so low, and their benefits so substantial, that I suggest you choose a system that makes sense in the context of your life, not on the basis of being 'natural'.

No contraceptive is foolproof, but new low-dose birth control pills are highly effective and seemingly protect against certain forms of cancer, too. Traditional reusable diaphragms are in general a good environmental choice, but many people find the necessary spermicides unpleasant to smell and taste and also a health worry.

Condoms are important because they protect against sexually transmitted diseases and tend to be widely available. They were originally made from biodegradable animal insides, but they are now made from almost indestructible latex and their new packaging rivals that of compact discs for eco unfriendliness. Flushed condoms pollute beaches and harm wildlife (birds think they're edible), so make sure you put them in the rubbish, not down the toilet.

The best eco alternative I've heard of is a cap similar to a diaphragm that is stored in a jar of clear honey. The honey is said to dehydrate sperm on contact and because it is antiseptic, the honey cap can stay in longer than a regular cap. The honey cap has to be fitted by a doctor and is said to have a 4 per cent failure rate, about the same as a diaphragm.

Dying Green

We have come to accept a medically monitored death in hospital, often isolated from family and friends, followed by cremation and floral tributes, as normal and even desirable. But a proper environment for dying and a restoration of the dignity of those who are near death are important parts of understanding and accepting ecological life cycles.

Beyond this, people who care about the natural world are reluctant to think of polluting it after their death with chemical treatment of the body, polluting smoke from a crematorium and non-biodegradable coffins. The Natural Death Centre publishes a guide to green burial *(see Resources)* and a number of councils around Britain have set aside land near existing graveyards for 'woodland cemeteries'.

There are surprising few legal restrictions on burial: you do not have to have a coffin, a gravestone, an undertaker or a religious ceremony. A person can choose to be buried in a biodegradable cardboard coffin or in a locally-woven woollen burial shroud. Woodland graves are generally unmarked, though sometimes a small plaque is posted. One such cemetery plants an oak sapling and several hundred bluebell bulbs on each grave and scatters wildflower seeds. Think of it – you can help to reforest Britain and make this land a green and pleasant one, long after your days of fighting motorway construction are over.

5

Leisure and Sport

Until recently, environmentalists haven't talked about sport. Displaying a passion for football or tennis was the equivalent, in terms of the rainforest, of Nero fiddling while Rome burned. Nor have they paid much attention to how we spend our leisure hours, except occasionally to criticise competitive games at school. You'll find far more information available about the environmental and health impact of buying GM-free food and organic plant food than about getting active to improve your immunity or the ecological impact of skiing or golf.

Nevertheless, I'm discussing active leisure – exercise and sport – here for two reasons. First, sport is a major world business and has a significant environmental impact. The aim of the Olympic Games, for instance, is co-operation and fellowship between nations – which are essential at this time of global ecological problems. The 2000 Sydney Games, in fact, were billed as the first 'green Olympics'. Secondly, physical activity is one of the most important components of a environmentally sound lifestyle, because it gets you involved in the world and aware of your body and your surroundings. It's probably more important than diet in keeping you healthy, too, and is essential to a strong immune system that can cope with all the challenges our modern world throws at us. And exercise gives a new twenty-first-century meaning to the term 'eco-activist'!

There's a growing interest in outdoor adventure activities,

including new sports like snowboarding and rollerblading, and new research continues to show the benefits of increased physical activity. These include an improved appearance, less painful periods, better memory, higher self-esteem and stronger bones. Human beings are meant, biologically, to be active. While it's impossible for most of us to change our sedentary jobs – it's a beautiful afternoon, but I'm sitting here in front of a computer, writing this book – we can reorient our leisure time to increase the amount of activity we get. We'll be healthier and happier, and far better able to cope with unavoidable exposure to air, water and other pollution.

Throughout human history, people have been trying to find ways to reduce physical labour. We're still doing it, with remote controls so we don't have to walk six feet to switch TV channels and light switches that we can clap on. The result is that throughout the developed world people are out of shape. It's no coincidence that the United States, the land of pizza delivery and drive-through banking, is the fattest country in the world and is getting fatter all the time. This shows what happens when your aim is to exert yourself as little as possible.

In past centuries it was hard work scrubbing clothes on the riverbank, grinding meat and ploughing fields. Getting around on horseback kept some people – including upper-class women – fit and ordinary people walked everywhere. We don't need to use our bodies the way our ancestors did, but think how ridiculous an aerobics class must seem to someone who gets all the exercise she needs hauling water from a well three miles away. Perhaps joggers should run on machines which would turn some of the energy they expend into electricity!

Immunity

One of the most important reasons to make regular physical activity part of eco living is that moderate exercise is the simplest, cheapest way to strengthen the immune system. While we can't avoid everything that might be or even that we know is harmful in our environment, if our immune systems are functioning well, our bodies can cope with a lot. After all, every one of us is exposed to hundreds of viruses and bacteria every day and we don't continually catch cold or get ill.

I have observed that friends who take regular exercise are healthier in general, and since I started walking a lot and doing yoga regularly a few years ago, I have almost stopped catching colds. This observation is confirmed by medical studies and doctors recommend regular moderate exercise to enhance your body's natural killer cell activity.

Studies have found that a simple regime of regular exercise has striking physical and psychological effects. Exercise boosts energy levels, tones muscles, decreases arthritic pain and chronic backache, and has proven anti-depressant effects. Experts even recommend walking for people suffering from chronic fatigue syndrome (ME) and severe depression, so just think what it can do for those of us suffering from ordinary inertia and job stress.

Q Exercise is especially important for women because it also reduces the risk of breast cancer, heart disease and osteoporosis.

Sport and the Environment

I don't know whether it's coincidence that the fewer health benefits you get from a sport, the more likely it is to be environmentally damaging. Motor sports, golf and downhill or Alpine skiing have all been criticised for ecological damage and none of them will make you fit or slim! If you love these sports, do what you can to encourage more environmentally benign approaches and also look at doing other activities to round out your sporting life.

Golf has a pristine image, but modern golf courses are often built on undeveloped land which was a healthy habitat for many animals, plants and insects. The manicured artificial landscape of most courses requires a huge input of chemical fertilisers (to produce perfectly even, bright green lawn), herbicides (to kill weeds in the green) and pesticides (to keep insects away). Golf courses also use huge amounts of water. After much criticism, this is beginning to change, and some courses now leave wild meadows and have reduced pesticide and water use.

Q A golf course in Thailand uses as much water as 60,000 villagers.

Alpine skiing is another popular sport that is environmentally damaging. We've come a long way from the simplicity of early skiing. Ski areas use huge amounts of energy, especially now that they make snow throughout a long season, and encourage road and air travel. Cross-country (Nordic) skiing, on the other hand, is a relatively benign winter sport. It's easy to take up, highly aerobic once you pick up speed and sociable too.

Motor sports – like jet skiing and snowmobiling – are polluting, noisy, damaging to wildlife and fuel intensive. Fortunately, there are dozens of exciting sports, old and new, that rely on human, wind and water power and can be done without impinging on delicate wilderness or aquatic environments.

TIPS: FOR CHOOSING SPORTING ACTIVITIES
- Think twice – and thrice – about a swimming pool. Home pools have significant negative environmental impact in water and energy use.
- Look for leisure activities you can enjoy without driving hundreds of miles. (And if you move, consider opportunities near your new home.)
- Choose a sailing boat or canoe over a motorboat or jet ski.
- Choose cross-country skiing over downhill.

>Nature Time

Sports centres and gyms can be terrific, giving us opportunities to work our muscles and forget about work. But the eco-activist looks for ways to explore and enjoy the natural world by being active outside. Of course it depends where you live, but even in cities there are some wonderful places to walk, cycle, run and play tennis or football. And even not so wonderful places can be fine – especially with the right companions. A chlorinated pool, for example, can be good preparation for holiday excursions where you can swim in a lake.

At its best, physical activity reconnects us with our physical being, and as an extension of that, helps us understand ourselves as part of the natural world. It's exhilarating to reach the top of a hill or feel your calf muscles burning after an extra mile. So get outside, whether you live – as I did for years – in south London or in a Yorkshire village!

The Fundamentals

A balanced fitness programme includes aerobic and anaerobic training, as well as proper nutrition. Here's a summary of these types of training, along with tips on the easiest ways to incorporate them into your life. I'm partial to activities that require little or no special equipment and don't take much time, but it's most important to find activities that you enjoy – and that don't put pressure on the environment.

>Aerobic Exercise

Also called 'cardiovascular exercise', this is the kind of workout that raises your heart rate and gets your lungs working hard for a sustained period of time. It doesn't have to be terribly strenuous – a brisk walk will do – but it does need to be regular and steady, and it's important at every age. Kids need to run and cycle and climb trees, and adults can play tennis or football or jog.

>Anaerobic or Resistance Exercise

All sports – except the kind you can do while holding a beer or smoking – provide both aerobic and anaerobic exercise. But many do not provide enough anaerobic activity to build strength. You'll feel and look better if you build strength, and if you're female you'll avoid osteoporosis, the bone loss that plagues older women. The myth that exercise will make women 'unfeminine' and muscle-bound is promoted by men who don't want to share the track or gym with us! Women do not have the hormones to develop big muscles and what you will get from serious resistance exercise is a shapely body (whatever size you are), greatly enhanced health and improved immunity.

>The First Resort

Walking is the first and maybe the best form of exercise. It provides all the aerobic benefit you need and costs almost nothing. It's easy to squeeze into a busy day and can be done in bits and pieces. Studies have found that regular walking is the single best way to lose weight, too.

It wasn't long ago that most people did a lot of walking, to do the shopping, pick up children from school or catch a bus to work. But as cars have proliferated, we walk less and less. So do our children. With a little reorganising, we can start walking again and reap many health benefits while reducing wear and tear on planet Earth.

You can walk alone, to get some precious time to reflect and regroup, or with a friend. My friend Valerie, a dancer, insists that when we walk we have a chance to catch up on our lives, and over the course of four or five miles we cover local gossip, new relationships and career plans. Walking should be brisk, to get your heart rate up, but you should be able to talk comfortably. All you need is a comfortable pair of shoes and appropriate clothing. I always wear sun block on my face and exposed neck, too. And walking can be done year round. To reap the most benefit, aim to walk steadily for at least 20 minutes three times a week.

Cycling is also a fun way to get around – in a city, it's an adrenalin rush, too. That can be good or bad, depending on how you feel about it. On the whole cycling is not such good exercise as walking because steady exercise is most beneficial and freewheeling down hills doesn't use any effort. Also, because cycles are so efficient at converting effort into motion, it's hard to go fast enough to get your pulse rate up to an ideal level.

In terms of low-tech aerobic activities that fit into almost anyone's lifestyle, running gets a high score. It isn't a good way to get around, however, because you can't carry things and you'll be sweaty at the end. Also, injury rates are much higher than with plain walking. Running is wonderful and I hope you'll try it, but everybody can walk.

Environmental Hazards

Water pollution is a problem for many sports people. Human sewage contaminates some beaches, and various industrial chemicals and agricultural run-off can make rivers and lakes dangerous. In one well-known case, dozens of athletes in a triathlon competition became ill, with some suffering long-term neurological damage as a result of microbacterial infection. You can reduce health risks by not swallowing water, not swimming when you have open cuts and avoiding swimming during or soon after extreme weather conditions.

It's obviously much more pleasant to exercise if you can breathe clean air. In a city, it's ideal to exercise early in the morning and at weekends, and of course you'll want to stay off main roads. Some cyclists wear masks to avoid breathing in the particulate from car exhaust. Whenever you can, take your exercise away from cars and industry, and remember that the air inside a sports centre may be just as polluted as the air outside – though the benefits of exercise far outweigh exposure to a little more air as you breathe more deeply.

Multiple Benefits

Exercise is a stress-reliever and certain forms of physical activity seem to give far more than toned biceps. These systems include yoga, *tai chi* and Pilates. I'm providing a quick résumé of these approaches here, but it's by no means an exhaustive list.

These activities are rewarding on many levels and are good ways to get moving because they teach you to be aware of your body. If you practise them as well as do regular walking for aerobic benefits, you'll soon find yourself ready to try more demanding outdoor activities with friends, your partner or children, or with a team.

>Yoga

Yoga is an ancient Indian system of physical and mental practice. It came to the West in the 1960s and has become increasingly popular since then. Originally it was seen as a rather introspective activity focused on stretching and meditation. In the 1990s, the picture changed as well-known actors and performers, including Madonna and Richard Gere, took up more vigorous new forms of yoga and announced that it was the best exercise they'd ever done. What has remained consistent is that most practitioners feel that they benefit spiritually or psychologically, as well as physically, from their practice.

Yoga is about as low tech as exercise gets. You simply need comfortable, loose clothing and a mat or towel. It can be learned from a book, but you'll get most benefit from going to a class. If you want gentle toning, try Hatha or Iyengar yoga (both systems can be practised to an advanced level, too). If you're interested in a more aerobic workout, look for Power or Astanga yoga.

>Tai Chi

Tai Chi is characterised by simple and graceful circular movements that are performed in a continuous flow and at a slow, even pace, and also by a strict composition in which lightness is integrated with firmness and tranquillity with solemnity. Along with other Chinese and Asian martial arts, it focuses on self-development and discipline, not competition. It is extremely hard work, though, much like some types of yoga, and highly fit people find themselves aching after their first session. You'll need to learn it from a teacher, but it can be practised anywhere with a little space and privacy.

>Pilates

Pilates is a physical training system developed in the 1920s by Joseph Pilates (1881–1967) and long used by dancers and actors because of the way it builds strength and shapes the body without adding bulk. Like yoga, which it is based on, Pilates develops a long, lean look and works a lot with the spine and stomach muscles.

Traditional Pilates is done in private lessons on special Pilates machines. It is very expensive. The system has become much more popular in the last couple of years, because proponents have developed exercises that can be done without expensive equipment, at home or in small classes.

TIPS: FOR EXERCISING

- Get a book or go to a sports centre or gym to get started. A perfectly adequate strength programme can be done at home, but you may want guidance and support to get started (if you have health concerns, do check with your doctor).
- There are running clubs all over the country, many with support for novice, older and female runners.
- Don't wear headphones. They are a safety hazard (you won't hear cars or other dangers) and also disconnect you from the outside world – eco living is about tuning in to your world.
- Drink plenty of water – plain tap water, filtered if necessary, rather than bottled water or sports drinks – before, during and after sports, to avoid cramp, muscle strain and fatigue.
- Wear the right shoes for impact activities and try to run on grass, dirt paths or a track.
- Warm up and cool down with five minutes' walking or even jogging in place.
- Wear the right clothing, shoes and reflective gear if you're out in the rain or after dark.

Extreme and Adventure Activities

Extreme sports are increasingly popular, both for spectators and participants. They are characterised by an apparent lack of rules and a focus on pushing the limits of danger and risk, and include such activities as mountain biking, whitewater rafting and snowboarding. The popularity of extreme sports with men and increasingly with younger women makes sense. We've eliminated almost all the physical risks that humans evolved with and there is little or no physical challenge in modern life. Both big companies and youth crime experts know the psychological and team-building benefits that can result from facing physical challenges and getting away from civilisation.

So, if you're looking for adventure, self-knowledge and the extreme challenge of working as part of a team, you may find yourself wearing a parachute or signing up for a kayaking holiday. Outward Bound and similar trips are designed for the inexperienced and are ideal if you haven't run 100 yards since school.

Q Eco activities depend as little as possible on planes or cars or buses, don't require vast amounts of new equipment and don't involve taking noise (mobile phones) or waste (disposable nappies) into unspoilt countryside or wilderness.

Hygiene in the Open Air

Human body waste is creating health problems in many wilderness areas. Before the 1970s, the protozoan cysts of Giardia and oocysts of Cryptosporidium – the bacteria that create havoc with tourists in certain parts of the developing world – were rare, but today they are considered a hazard everywhere on the planet. The evidence of human presence is making outdoor activities less pleasant, and less safe, for everyone.

Wilderness experience is precious and if you're really going to get back to nature you need to develop a rugged attitude towards human biology. Urine is almost sterile and disappears immediately, but faecal waste and menstrual products need to be dealt with properly when you are far from plumbing and drains. Ecologically aware rock climbers use 'carryout' containers – plastic pots or World War II ammunition cans that travel in empty and out full. Even casual ramblers should keep these tips in mind:

- Use a private spot at least 150 feet from streams or lakes and above the high water line.
- Dig a hole 6 to 8 inches deep, in humousy soil if possible. Avid outdoors people carry an old trowel.
- Loo paper will decompose if buried, but experts recommend carrying or 'packing' it out. Experiment with natural wiping materials: dead grasses or leaves, even snow.

- Cover the hole (those hardy experts also recommend stirring, with a handy stick, before pushing the earth back).
- If you have to dig a group hole, it should be shallow and long and well away from water sources.
- Ritualise hand washing after visiting the WC and always before eating.
- For women: many sanitary products are part plastic, which should never be left behind. If you're menstruating on a wilderness trip, you have two options: pack it out or burn it.
- For parents: disposable nappies must be packed out and cloth nappies should be washed in a basin well away from water sources.
- Whatever you pack out should be flushed, never put into the rubbish.

6

The Three Rs

The three Rs, in an environmental context, are: reduce, reuse and recycle. Recycling continues to be high on the environmental agenda and bottle banks are increasingly common. Critics, however, contend that the emphasis on recycling draws attention away from the more significant steps we should be taking: reducing packaging and switching to reuse systems such as bottle refilling. Also, stories continue to surface about the inability of industry to cope with the quantities of recycling materials.

There is a model for 100 per cent recycling without polluting byproducts: Nature itself. Likewise, our goal has to be products and methods that will create no pollution – either when they are made, when we use or wear them, or when they are no longer wanted. This goal don't change the way we go about recycling right now, but our target should be to reuse and recycle everything, so there is no such thing as waste or rubbish.

Signs of the nascent eco economy are already around us. The most creative designers today are working on fabrics and packaging that will be functional, beautiful and completely Earth-friendly. Some companies are supplying services rather than goods – leasing copying machines, floor tiles, even carpets, and taking them back for recycling or remanufacture as needed. This gives them an incentive to design equipment to last and also to have parts that can be reused in new machines. Other industries are setting up systems to sell their waste to those could can use it, rather than dumping it into landfills or the ocean.

While this chapter will concentrate on *materials* that pass through our hands, keep in mind that there are other things we use, too. Reducing energy use is covered in Chapters 7, 11 and 12. Reducing water use is also vital. Water tables are falling on every continent as aquifers are being drained by agricultural, industrial and consumer use. Drought is becoming more common, even in Britain. Water conservation is discussed in Chapters 1 and 10.

Q It may well be more important to buy recycled products than to recycle items yourself, because successful recycling depends on consumer demand. Choose things made from 'post-consumer' paper or plastic.

Our World of Waste

Recycling and reuse have always been part of local economies. In the past, everything was put to good use – much great country cooking is the result of our grandmothers' determination to waste nothing. It is only during the past few decades that we have ignored the resource potential of things we no longer need. Overflowing bins and a growing waste problem are the result, with black bags piled along city streets and litter festooning country hedgerows.

However, times are changing and there is an increased awareness of the environmental consequences of waste. There have been explosions of methane gas which has leaked from landfill tips (methane is a potent contributor to global warming), while toxic leachate fluid seeping from a tip can contaminate groundwater. As a result of these factors and the increased distance rubbish has to be transported from urban regions, rubbish collection and landfill costs are rising dramatically.

Economic pressures are combining with environmental concerns to encourage new approaches.

Most environmental specialists and consumer groups believe that greater effort should be put into reducing the amount of domestic waste by forcing manufacturers to reduce packaging, by developing refill systems (sometimes called 'precycling'), and by developing local composting schemes for the 20 per cent of domestic waste which is biodegradable vegetable material.

>Incineration

Incineration is the most expensive way of handling waste and it destroys natural resources. It has become a nightmare problem in communities around the globe, especially as new research on dioxin and other chemical hazards has shown the danger presented by even well-managed incineration facilities. There have been attempts by the incinerator industry in the US to use ash for roadbeds and concrete building blocks, but the heavy metals, dioxins and furans in incinerator waste are permanent and need to be treated much like the waste from nuclear power stations. (Technical improvements won't help: better air pollution control would mean more toxic ash.)

>Petrochemicals

Products made from petroleum (natural oil) resources include plastics, synthetic fabrics, newsprint and a nearly infinite array of other common items. Plastics are perhaps the most pernicious. They can be water-resistant, light and almost unbreakable – and they are cheap. The trouble is that they last for ever, are difficult to recycle, there are toxicity problems associated with many of them and dangerous dioxins are given off when they are incinerated.

Toxic waste from the petrochemical industry is a leading source of world pollution (oil spills, air and water pollution from petrol stations, and leachate contamination of groundwater from landfill sites), but petrochemicals surround us. The keyboard I am typing on, the soles of my boots and the switch on my desk lamp are all made from plastics which have been developed from petroleum. Even candles are made from petroleum-derived wax. As an alternative, use beeswax candles or revive an ancient mode of lighting with an oil lamp. Choose rattan wastebaskets, paper packaging, natural fibre clothing and cosmetics containing minimal petrochemicals.

>Toxic Waste

Toxic waste is a growing problem in the industrialised world and domestic rubbish also has its share of toxic contaminants. Think how casually we throw away used batteries, an old box of moth balls or a couple of cans of dried-up paint.

The main thing we can do, individually, is to stop using as many toxic products as possible and to encourage the production of benign alternatives. Some councils have toxic waste collection points and it's most important not to allow these materials to enter the water system; seal them and put them into the collection bin for landfill disposal. Used motor oil can be recycled and should be taken to a garage which collects it. Some car accessories shops collect used oil and antifreeze for reprocessing.

Q Batteries contain a wide variety of toxic substances and manufacturing them takes fifty times more energy than they hold. If you do use batteries, get a recharger. Used batteries should be treated as toxic waste.

Reduce

To reduce the total amount of waste we produce we need to rethink our buying, particularly the way we expect goods to be packaged. Try not to buy things you're not sure you need and if you are trying something new, start with a sample or a small size. Buy only things you love (and will go on loving). If in doubt, come back another day.

Apply some ingenuity before rushing out to buy something. Style often comes from using creativity rather than cash. Why buy curtain poles if you can trim a few beautiful ash branches to use instead?

>Energy Use

Energy costs. The price of everything we buy includes a percentage for the energy needed to produce and transport it. As globalisation continues and the things we buy come from further away, energy costs increase. In addition, the chemical-based agriculture that produces most of our food as well as raw materials for fabrics and many other products is extremely energy-intensive. Energy is used to produce fertilisers and pesticides – often made from petrochemicals – and to manufacture and run mechanical equipment. Large-scale agriculture uses energy for processing, packaging, storage and transportation. Throw in the energy used to get you to the supermarket and you'll see that our purchases are directly influencing the atmosphere and contributing to global warming.

>Water

Another way that almost anything you buy has an impact on the environment is the amount of clean water required to make it. Think of producing a meal: how much heating, cooling and cleaning does it take? In the same way, producing paper, metal, paint, cloth, etc. requires water. Agriculture requires huge amounts of water.

In spite of the fact that Earth is the water planet, clean water is becoming increasingly scarce – perhaps more scarce than energy sources, which were considered the most important resource in the 1970s. We're still producing oil, and more oil is being discovered. Xiching, China's westernmost state, is thought to have more oil reserves than the entire USA. The problem with oil is that burning it leads to global warming, so we should if possible leave it in the ground. Water is a different and more perplexing problem. We have plenty of water, yet we don't have it where it is needed, and the way we use it is inefficient and wasteful.

>Packaging

Packaging performs a number of functions. It protects a product during transport and storage, keeps it dry, enables it to be boxed or stacked neatly, displays it to advantage, makes it easy to carry or use, and conveys information. But packaging is also used as an advertising medium and as a way to increase the prominence of items on display. Packaging isn't free. Rubbish disposal isn't either. The UK packaging industry uses 39 million tonnes of materials each year, for which we pay £5,000 million.

The tradeoffs are not always obvious, either. Replacing a thin layer of plastic wrapping with masses of paper wrapping is not necessarily good for the environment. Many traditional practices were eco friendly. Thai women traditionally wrap food in banana leaves and in Britain burdock (or butterbur) leaves were used for the same purpose. Manufacturers need to come up with similarly low-impact materials.

The Women's Environmental Network has run a 'Wrap It Up' campaign and produced 'Send It Back' labels to post superfluous packaging back to manufacturers or shops, challenging them to justify excessive or inappropriate packaging. Contact them for more information and action packs *(see Resources)*.

Another thing to think of when throwing packaging away is the potential danger to wildlife. Animals can be caught in plastic netting and deer have been known to die as the result of swallowing plastic bags. The plastic rings which hold drinks packs together can be lethal too.

TIPS: FOR ECO PACKAGING

- Buy in bulk.
- Cut down on canned and bottled food.
- Buy in returnable/refillable containers.
- Choose products such as washing liquid packed in bags or refill packs.
- Look for concentrated products.
- Avoid 'mixed' packaging (e.g. juice boxes, aerosols, bubble packs).
- Choose paper wrapping over plastic.
- Carry your own shopping bags or use the store's own boxes. (Choosing a plastic carrier bag is not, contrary to popular opinion, the worst of environmental sins – a cloth or string bag is the best choice, but don't lose sleep over this issue.)

>Plastics

Plastics are made from petrochemicals, in polluting factories. A single scrap of wrapping or a disposable razor will sit in a landfill site for thousands and thousands of years. When burned, plastics create toxic gases and some plastics give off chemicals that can cause cancer or mess up your hormones. Synthetic fabrics continually give off fine fibres which go into the air and have been associated with the rise in juvenile asthma and allergies.

All plastic should be part of an endless recycling loop, but many environmentalists believe that some plastics, especially PVC (polyvinyl chloride), should be phased out entirely. PVC, a soft plastic, is used in clingfilm, shower curtains, plastic bags and hundreds of everyday items. It is thought to cause cancer, birth defects, skin diseases and liver dysfunction as well as many other health problems, and some major manufacturers have pledged to eliminate its use, especially in children's toys and equipment.

TIPS: FOR USING PLASTIC

Avoid food coming into direct contact with soft plastics.
- Buy food packed in glass, paper or natural cellophane.
- Do not drink hot drinks from polystyrene cups.
- Use plastic-free food wrapping or, preferably, store food in reusable containers.
- Never microwave food in plastic containers.
- Let new plastic items air outside or in an unused room until any noticeable smell has disappeared.

>Paper

We are profligate with paper and forget that in most of the world it is a precious commodity. Over a third of the waste in the average landfill site is paper, although this is an excellent material for recycling.

Paper production consumes large quantities of energy and water, and the bleaches, dyes and other chemicals used contribute to air and water pollution, as well as posing a danger to human health. The plantations of fast-growing conifers which provide most of our paper pulp also lead to the degradation of precious countryside and the loss of important wildlife habitats.

TIPS: FOR SAVING PAPER

- Consider cutting down on the number of papers you buy. How many of us claim never to have time to read a book, but spend many hours each month reading the paper, perhaps one each morning and evening, as much for entertainment as for news?
- Have your name removed from solicitation lists (*see Resources for the Mailing Preference Service, which can have your name taken off participating companies' mailing lists*). Why not prepare a photocopied note saying that because you are concerned about the environment and paper waste, you do not want your name sold to any other firm? Enclose a copy whenever you join an organisation or subscribe to a magazine.
- Cut attractive cards in half and use the front as a postcard next time you need to drop a note to a friend.
- Save sheets of paper which have been used on one side for anything from shopping lists to interoffice notes.
- Use the envelope reuse labels which are available.
- Buy products made from recycled paper.

>Down with Disposables

Many common household articles have been specifically designed to be disposable. Usually made from paper or plastic, they place unnecessarily heavy demands on natural wood and oil resources. There are times when modern disposables are handy, but why not try some of the following:

- *Paper towels:* Use terry towels for your hands and a dishcloth for the work top. Drain fried food on brown paper bags.
- *Sponges:* Cotton or linen dishcloths last much longer than sponges. Real cellulose sponges are a biodegradable choice.
- *Disposable cleaning cloths:* Cotton cleaning rags cut from old sheets or old clothes. Linen is good for windows.
- *Paper napkins:* Cloth napkins made of sturdy cotton fabric which does not need to be ironed. I make my own and have bought pretty ones in France.
- *Aluminium foil and plastic wrap:* Cover baking dishes with an upended pie plate or baking tray and a bowl with a saucer.
- *Plastic bags:* Wash and reuse. Stick them over an empty wine bottle to dry.
- *Coffee filters:* Reusable gold or hemp filter, or a cafetière. Try loose tea instead of teabags.
- *Paper and polystyrene cups and paper plates:* Keep a set of older dishes for use in the garden or on picnics. If you travel by car, keep several mugs and some cutlery in a basket, ready for impromptu picnics.
- *Bin liners:* Line bins with sheets of newspaper, or those plastic carrier bags you can't bring yourself to throw away. Most of your rubbish will be dry if you compost food scraps *(see Chapter 10)*.
- *Carrier bags:* Use durable canvas shopping bags or string bags.
- *Disposable nappies:* For information about switching to cloth nappies, turn to page 184.
- *Facial tissues:* Cotton handkerchiefs are a nice alternative.

Reuse

The kind of reuse discussed above – refill systems, for example – are not the only ways to give the things we use and buy a longer life. You can also buy and restore old items, and repair clothing and furniture. 'Recycling' generally means the reprocessing of an industrially-produced material like glass or metal. But a more cost-effective form of recycling is to reuse things. Containers can and should be designed for reuse. The obvious example is the British pint of milk: each bottle is filled an average of twelve times.

>Things That Last

Think about durability and repairability when you shop. The shoddy impermanence of much of what we buy makes it difficult to maintain things through a lifetime. Professional repair services are more difficult to find than they used to be and it is often more expensive to have mass-produced goods repaired than to buy new ones.

Buying higher quality and more costly items is an incentive to choose carefully and to make things last. A fountain pen will outlast dozens of plastic biros and is a pleasure to write with. A really good piece of clothing might last fifty years. Furniture, assuming that it is well made in the first place, can last for centuries. Most ordinary household mugs and glasses are easy to break, and you'll get better wear by buying things designed for restaurant and hotel use. These range from simple and serviceable to elegant. Look in catering shops, which are also a source of heavy cooking pans and utensils.

>Donations

Set up a system for sorting things you don't need or want, whether rubbish or last year's orange trousers. It's a bit of a psychological shift to organise what's going out of your home the same way you organise what's coming in, but once you have a system in place it's very easy to carry on and you'll save some money as well as have a tidier place to live.

- Ensure that anything you pass on is clean and still useful. Really worn clothing is better turned into dustcloths.
- Pin sets of clothing and bag articles which should stay together.
- Do not remove buttons.
- Attach a note to old appliances or electronic equipment to say whether they work or need certain repairs.
- Save household items such as yoghurt pots and egg cartons for schools and play groups.
- Be creative: our local doctors' office was delighted with a large bundle of fairly current magazines.

TIPS: FOR REPAIRING

- Love your tools and learn to take care of them. It helps to buy the best.
- Buy things which can be repaired and for which you can buy replacement parts. Ask about servicing when you buy.
- Read the instructions. These are not inspiring pieces of literature, but it's well worth coming to grips with your tools' terminology and structure.
- Before calling for help, make an effort to solve the problem yourself.
- Assemble a reference shelf: a folder with all the instruction leaflets for appliances and electronic equipment, as well as basic books. The *Reader's Digest* guides are good, and I collect old repair manuals to help me repair secondhand purchases like my faithful 1950s toaster.

Recycle

At last we reach the third R: recycle. Opportunities for recycling vary considerably. If you don't already know about what's available in your area, look in your phone book for 'Recycling Facilities' listings. These provide guidance about bottles, cans, newspapers, magazines, car batteries and motor oil, old clothes and even household appliances.

Once you are organised, you'll be able to cope with the vagaries of today's recycling and be ready for the more efficient schemes which are coming. We will all then adopt a more appreciative attitude towards the things which pass through our hands – seeing them as resources, not rubbish.

Recycling should be easy, unobtrusive and routine. Work out a neat, convenient system for sorting types of waste. Once you get used to recycling, dropping coffee grounds into the same container as newspapers and last night's wine bottle will seem messy and unpleasant, as well as wasteful. It helps to arrange things so that you can separate and store everything, except perhaps bulky newspapers, in one spot. Here are a few more ideas:

- Make your system attractive, a permanent part of your kitchen. A sturdy pine crate or a plastic children's toy box will last a long time.
- Use bins or boxes, not plastic bags.
- Use the largest containers that space allows and you can carry. You shouldn't have to move or empty a bin, except for kitchen waste, more than once a week.
- Choose containers which are easy to carry, empty and clean. This is especially important with wet waste and heavy glass.
- Place the containers as near as possible to site of use. Most recyclables should be stored, at least temporarily, in the kitchen, though you may want to put a big bin (or an attractive basket) for newspapers in the sitting room.
- Take up as little floor space as possible, with stackable bins or boxes on shelves, but ensure that every bin is in position for a quick toss.
- Label containers to make sorting easy for your family and

guests (use cut-out magazine illustrations to help small children).

- Include a space for items you intend to donate.

TIPS: FOR KITCHEN COMPOSTING

- Use a galvanised metal or stainless steel container, as these can be sterilised with boiling water.
- Line the compost container with newspaper for easy emptying.
- Spread a piece of newspaper before you start chopping. When you have finished, gather up the edges and put the whole thing in the compost bin.
- Try composting with worms. This may sound strange, but the bins are compact and efficient and great fun for children. Properly managed, the bins do not smell because the garbage is digested before it can rot. They can even be kept in a flat, and the end result is a rich black material which can be used in the garden or for potted plants. (*See Chapter 10 and Resources for more information.*)

>Strategies for the Future

Recycling of materials, from paper to plastic to leaves and kitchen waste, should be part of an organised community effort. Glass is far better reused than recycled, and this would become easier for both consumers and manufacturers if there were standard sizes for all bottles and jars. Parts and materials from all kinds of manufactured goods can be reused or recycled into new parts. Rank Xerox is one company at the forefront of this industrial recycling, stripping old equipment down and rebuilding new machines with restored and recycled components. Remanufacturing is an essential component in recycling strategies.

The EU has plans to require manufacturers and retailers to recover 90 per cent of packaging for recycling and the British government is set to impose recycling costs on industry as well. In Germany, consumers have the right to return packaging and demand that it be recycled by manufacturers.

7

Your Comfort Zone

Part of the cost of each item we buy is the energy which has been used to make it. Crisps have to be fried and iron ore has to be smelted to make steel for bicycle chains. Chemical farming techniques are energy-intensive because of the equipment used and because man-made fertilisers and pesticides are made from petroleum derivatives. Added to these is the energy needed for packaging and transport. As long as we use more than we generate or can renew, conventional sources of power won't last for more than a few generations.

Not only this, but most of the world's commercial energy is provided by fossil fuels – coal, oil and natural gas. When they are burned, carbon dioxide (CO_2) is released – the primary cause of the greenhouse effect. The amount of CO_2 in the atmosphere is now more than 15 per cent higher than in pre-industrial times and could easily double within the next 50–100 years. The Meteorological Office predicts a 5.2°C rise in global temperatures, which will lead to extensive flooding around the world and cause increasing storm damage to homes and agriculture.

The only known solution to global warming is to reduce the combustion of fossil fuels. World-wide energy efficiency is the only way to avoid the worst climatic effects.

Saving energy can seem a fussy chore, but in fact it's an area where some of the most exciting environmental initiatives are taking place. Roughly a third of CO_2 emissions come from industry, a third from transportation and the remaining third is divided between the commercial sector and residences. On average, each of us is responsible for some 50 *tonnes* of carbon dioxide every year! There are hundreds of things we can do to cut our personal use of energy and new technologies have astonishing potential for reducing overall energy use.

Emissions of carbon declined slightly in 1998 as a result of improved energy efficiency and falling coal use. At the same time, the world economy expanded – evidence that we can do good and live well at the same time.

TIPS: FOR REDUCING YOUR CARBON CONTRIBUTION

- Choose the smallest home that is reasonable for you or your family. Consider sharing or renting out excess space.
- Minimise your heating, cooling and hot water costs.
- Maintain efficient lighting and appliances.
- Use non-electrical equipment whenever possible.
- Buy certified organic produce (organic food is grown without energy-intensive chemicals).
- Plant trees, shrubs, flowers and vegetable (plants absorb carbon from the air).
- Use local shops and ask for locally grown products.
- Choose a power company that offers renewable energy – more options are coming and Friends of the Earth can help now with a list of greener electricity companies *(see Resources)*.

The Energy-Efficient Home

Our buildings are the most wasteful energy users in industrial countries. Turning down the heat and insulating the attic may seem mundane, but these steps are important and there are many others that you can take.

Architects are increasingly conscious of energy-efficient design. There are a number of model building projects around the country where energy use is as little as a quarter of that in similar but conventionally built houses, thanks to advance insulation and materials and careful orientation. We can also choose energy-efficient appliances and products.

Better home insulation led to awareness of the dangers of combustion by-products, which include formaldehyde, nitrogen dioxide, sulphur dioxide and a host of other vapours and gases, because in a well-insulated house they invariably build up more than in a traditional draughty British home. Contrary to expectation, studies have found that colds and 'flu are less likely in draughty buildings. This may be because there is a build up of viruses in well-sealed buildings or because fresh air is needed to keep our immune systems functioning effectively *(see also Chapter 4)*.

A high-tech super-insulated building will need mechanical ventilation, and indoor air pollution control will be essential. Be especially careful to ensure that gas appliances have plenty of ventilation – to the outside! – while in operation. They must be correctly adjusted in order to burn efficiently. In the summer, a small ceiling fan helps to keep the place cool and in winter it circulates the warm air which would otherwise rise to the top of the room and stay there.

>Choose your Fuels

Using electricity for 'low-grade' energy such as domestic heating and hot water is wasteful because it is produced in power stations which burn large quantities of coal or oil to produce it and are, at best, only 35 per cent efficient. (An open coal fire, by contrast, is 20 per cent efficient, ie 80 per cent of the heat goes up the chimney.) When we heat by electricity, we lose over 90 per cent of the fuel's primary energy because of the inefficiency of the transmission systems and electrical appliances, so electricity is even less efficient than an open fire.

Gas is the best fuel for heating space and hot water, which makes up 80 per cent of home energy use, but the ultimate source of energy for space heating is the sun, a renewable 'fuel'.

Q Almost fifteen years after the world's worst nuclear disaster, the 1986 explosion at the Chernobyl power station in the Ukraine, some Welsh sheep (grazing on hillsides 1,500 miles from Chernobyl) are still classified as radioactive. Nuclear power is being phased out in some countries and is at a standstill in the United States.

While coal and oil supplies were laid down millions of years ago and are limited – as well as being the primary cause of global warming – renewable energy sources can be indefinitely sustained and do not create pollution or cause climate change. There are a wide variety of potential energy sources: sunlight, wind, flowing water, wood and plants. The tapping of renewable sources of energy has made remarkable strides over the past decade, even without anything like the measure of support enjoyed by conventional and nuclear power supplies. They are particularly suitable for the small-scale local projects recommended by many energy researchers.

Small does not mean inefficient. In fact, huge electricity-generating plants have turned out to be far less efficient than their creators envisaged fifty years ago. A healthy trend for energy companies is to think of 'energy portfolios'. Rather than rely entirely on one source, energy companies are developing a variety of energy sources and innovative policy proposals call for a gradually increasing proportion to be renewable resources, until we switch over entirely to renewables.

Even urban homes can take advantage of solar energy for heating and very simple systems are available which will provide hot tap water throughout much of the year. Check with the Centre for Alternative Technology for details *(see Resources)*.

>Simple Solar Power

If you want to use renewable energy, you could tackle something like solar panels or a wind-generator, but the simplest, cheapest form available to us is 'passive' solar heating. This means making maximum use of the sunlight which falls on your home. It works on a few simple principles.

TIPS: FOR USING SOLAR POWER

- Have large south-facing windows and smaller ones in north-facing rooms to avoid excessive heat loss there.
- Leave curtains open throughout the daylight hours, but close them promptly when it gets dark.
- Don't use net curtains, especially on south-facing windows.
- Remember that dark colours absorb sunlight (and heat), while light colours reflect it.
- Take advantage of the thermal inertia of building materials. A brick floor will absorb heat from the sun during the day and give it off through the evening, just as a brick garden wall is perfect for espaliered fruit because of the way it retains warmth.
- Conservatories are an ideal source of passive solar heat and can make a substantial contribution towards warming your home, as well as providing an extra room. Choose a south- or west-facing site if possible, out of the wind (you can plant windbreak trees or shrubs). Double-glazing will help to eliminate any need for heating, and you'll need blinds and ventilation for hot weather.
- More substantial design alterations are possible. For referral to an architect, contact the Ecological Design Association.

Comfort Zones

We have become engrossed in creating 'thermally stress-free environments' – central heating in winter and air conditioning in summer – on the assumption that constant temperature is desirable. In fact, the most pleasing – and ecological – solution is to create pools of warmth and pools of light. Humans need contrast and variety, and appropriate seasonal variation – not the craziness of the United States, where offices are heated to 75°F in the winter and cooled to 65°F in the summer!

>Keeping Warm

The easiest way to save energy at home without loss of comfort is to heat only the rooms you're using, and to warm rooms appropriately. An office should be cool enough to promote alertness, but you will want a warm bathroom while showering.

In general, the most comfortable heating for human beings is a combination of convected and radiant heat, something built into us by our evolution in the open air. Examples of this combination are sitting in warm sunshine on a mild spring day or in front of a glowing fire in a fairly cool room.

Your personal comfort depends on the rate at which your body loses heat to the air and this depends in part on the surface temperature of the objects around you. Although your body conducts some heat to the air, most of its heat is lost through radiation, just like a radiator. Radiation takes place through space, from one solid object to another, so the rate of radiation has to do mainly with the temperature of walls, floors and furniture, not the temperature of the air (which is what thermostats measure). Using plenty of natural, thermally neutral materials such as wood, cork and fabric – rather than brick and tile, enamelled steel and glass, which heat and cool readily – will enable you to maintain a more even, comfortable environment. The proper balance is a radiant temperature about 2°F higher than the air temperature. This simply means keeping room temperature quite low and having a heat source like a stove or an open fire, especially in rooms where people gather in cold weather.

TIPS: FOR KEEPING WARM

- Do a little exercise to warm yourself up on cold mornings.
- Wear wool.
- Dress in lots of layers. It can be useful to wear a thin synthetic layer next to your skin, under wool or cotton. Sweat 'wicks' through the synthetic fabric, away from your skin.
- Use and enjoy good old-fashioned warming methods like soft car blankets to wrap up in when you are sitting at home in the evening.
- Use a hot water bottle instead of an electric blanket – old-fashioned and wonderfully cosy (my kids love them). Even easier is a soft cloth bag – or a sock! – filled with rice or barley. Heat it for three minutes in the microwave and use it in bed or on a sore neck. Because it's flexible, you can drape it in just the right place. (These bags can also be frozen and used on strained muscles.)
- Thick cotton flannel sheets make the bed feel warmer and a wool blanket under the sheet helps it warm up too.

>Keeping Cool

Air conditioning has become a fact of life in Britain, a trend that is highly worrisome in terms of our energy use. In the United States heatwaves have led to series of power cuts because of high energy demand.

Air conditioning is also a problem in that it cuts us off from natural light and air, and does not allow or encourage our bodies to adapt to heat. Changes in temperature are a form of natural stimulus which we need to stay tuned to the environment around us – to stay healthy, in fact.

The need for air conditioning can be obviated by a number of simple architectural devices that are part of green home planning. Heat is a particular problem in urban areas, where wide paved streets act as heat collectors. Narrower streets with plenty of room for trees can reduce the need for air conditioning. Trees provide shade and cool the air by means of evaporation through transpiration, acting as natural air conditioners. Plant deciduous trees on the sunny side of your house; US research has shown that doing so can reduce air-conditioning costs by one third.

TIPS: FOR KEEPING COOL

- Dress for the heat in loose, light clothing. A sheer dress is more comfortable than tight shorts – think of a sari. Avoid synthetic fabrics. Cotton and linen may wrinkle, but are infinitely more comfortable.
- Spray yourself with spring water, sprinkle water on your head, wet your clothes or go swimming.
- Open windows at night and close them during the day. Keep the curtains closed while the sun is shining directly on the windows. Outdoor planting can provide welcome shade during warm summer months.
- Ensure that there is plenty of air movement, either by cross ventilation or an electric fan. This is an old-fashioned solution from the Deep South.
- A dampened curtain or sheet hung near a breezy window or in front of an electric fan will cool the air.
- Use a hand fan.

Heating and Hot Water Systems

TIPS: ON HEATING AND HOT WATER SYSTEMS

- Use a timer. New ones with electronic programming allow you different settings for different days, and to time heating and water separately.
- Fit thermostatic valves to radiators and use room thermostats. The hot water cylinder needs a thermostat too.
- Radiators should be placed on interior walls, contrary to the usual pattern – which is intended to warm window draughts before they enter the room.
- If you have radiators on external walls, paste sheets of aluminium foil (shiny side facing you) onto the wall behind them.
- Shelves above radiators direct warm air into the room rather than allowing it to rise to the ceiling: a layer of aluminium foil on the underside of the shelf makes this more efficient (you can purchase ready-made deflective shelves).
- If your ceilings are very high, consider building a platform area to take advantage of the warm air near the ceiling, and increase your living space at the same time.

- When installing a new central heating and hot water system, look at versions which run directly off the mains. They can be cheaper to run, give better water pressure and mean that you do not need water tanks (thus gaining storage space).
- If you have a hot water tank, lag it properly and use the heat it still gives off for an airing cupboard.

TIPS: FOR INSULATION

- Fitted double-glazing is expensive, inflexible and resource intensive. Secondary double-glazing (detachable in case of fire), however, can be installed for a fairly small amount of money. A more attractive and permanent solution is using double-pane glass in existing window frames.
- Heavy curtains are cheaper than double-glazing, easier to manoeuvre and look elegant. You can buy special lining fabric, aluminium or plastic-coated, for extra insulation.
- Shutters are even more effective than curtains. They are often boarded over in older houses, and it's worth taking a look in case you have some. If they have been removed, replace them with appropriate ones from a salvage firm or with new ones made up by a joiner.
- Loft insulation will cut your fuel bills and there may even be a grant available to help with the cost. Use mineral fibre, vermiculite chips or cellulose fibre rather than synthetic materials and make sure that insulation goes over your cold water tank to prevent it freezing.
- Consider cavity wall insulation – not urea-formaldehyde foam, which has been banned in the US because of health effects, but mineral fibre or cellulose.
- Hot water tanks need a warm jacket (the pay-back period on this is only a couple of months). Get a large size and fit it over the old thin one. You can also pad it with the same mineral fibre used in the loft, before putting the jacket on.
- Water pipes should be wrapped, too.
- Floors are insulated by carpeting and sheet flooring, but you can improve on this with thick fibre underlay, a layer of newspapers under the underlay or directly under linoleum (choose old-fashioned natural resin linoleum).

TIPS: FOR DRAUGHTPROOFING

- Stuffed draught excluders are an easy and cheap way to prevent draughts under doors.
- Hang curtains or thick quilts over windows and doors.
- Use lots of rugs on board floors.
- Ensure that windows are well caulked and weatherstrip window frames. Choose the more expensive, durable putty instead of adhesive foam, which disintegrates after a year or two. DIY stores have a wide range. Brass strip is durable and quite attractive, though not so easy to find as the cheaper types.
- Open doors as infrequently as possible in cold weather. Put spring-pull closing devices on doors that need to be kept closed.
- Chimneys have to be well ventilated in order to draw properly but an unused fireplace can be very draughty. (a) Install an efficient stove; (b) brick it up, incorporating air bricks as required; or (c) block it up with a fitted frame covered with board, with holes to allow some air through.

Lighting

Ordinary light bulbs have been called 'electric space heaters that give off a little light'. Put compact fluorescent light bulbs in your three most-used lights – they produce the same light for about a quarter of the energy of ordinary light bulbs and last eight times longer. You save £50–100 over the bulbs' lifetime (up to 10 years) and keep tonnes of carbon dioxide out of the atmosphere. The government's Energy Saving Trust provides some subsidies for the bulbs, available at superstores throughout the country. Visit the Energy Saving Trust website (www.est.org.uk) for more information.

8

Clean Space

I get more complaints about greener cleaners than any other aspect of eco living. They're expensive, people say, or they don't work: often both. Their results are obvious, too, unlike some of the other things that are part of eco living. Cleaners are a real test, because you can see right away whether a spot came out of that new white cotton shirt or the new window cleaner leaves ghostly streaks on your bathroom mirror.

Old-fashioned methods – often touted by environmentalists – were laborious and often used hazardous chemicals. Twenty-first-century eco living requires twenty-first-century cleaning methods. This means using our brains instead of using chemicals that pollute our rivers and reduce our immunity to illness. We also need products and techniques that everyone in a household can use.

Maybe it's true that you could have a sparkling house using nothing but plain soap and water, but I'm not going to try! Only the other day I read, 'you can do almost all your household cleaning and laundry with such safe and basic ingredients as lemon juice, baking soda, vinegar, borax, salt and olive oil.' Shipping Mediterranean or tropical foods like lemons and olive oil to Britain to use as cleaning products is far from ecological. Can you really imagine squeezing lemons to bleach your wash?

I rate vinegar and water highly for some purposes. But in some cases, the ecological choice is to buy your favourite commercial product in the largest container possible, a concentrated version if that's available, and then to use it sparingly.

The advantages of using only natural cleaning products include the facts that you won't have an itchy nose from chemical fumes and you can involve children in your Saturday morning work (and *they* think washing the front of cabinets is fun!) If you're the one responsible for stocking the cleaning cupboard, choose carefully. Many ideas follow. For information on cleaning clothes, see pages 42–6, and for ideas about washing dishes, see page 101. Here we'll concentrate on the basics of a clean, fresh-smelling, safe home.

First Principles

A recent study found that household cleaners do a lot of damage to the environment in terms of the money spent on them. Many cleaners also pollute our indoor air environment and thus may be even more damaging to our health – as we breathe in their fumes in a closed environment – than to the world outside. It's easy to make changes, though. Before we get into specifics, here are some general principles:

TIPS: FOR CLEANING

- Use up your old cleaners or give them away to someone who will use them. (Don't throw them out or pour them down the drain.)
- Store and use products carefully. Some natural cleaners can be skin irritants and should be kept out of children's reach.
- Avoid products with lengthy warning labels.
- Buy concentrated products in large containers. You can pour liquids into smaller bottles at home.
- Reduce the cleaning, polishing and spot removal you have to do by planning ahead. Choose patterned carpets and fabrics that won't show every spot, put small decorative objects into a glass-fronted cupboard and if you have pets, choose colours that co-ordinate with your pet's fur.

- Reduce the dirt that gets into your house by installing good mats both outside and inside the main doors. Carpets last longer if they are kept clean – it's the abrasiveness of dirt, rather than traffic, which does most of the damage.
- Take your shoes off at the door, to reduce the need to clean.
- Try water, the first and best cleaner. Rather than grinding away at the pudding batter that has dried onto your cooker, simply wet it. After 10 minutes, wipe it up. This principle works on clothes and floors, as well as on dishes.

Natural Disinfectants: Germ-free Living?

Germs are just bacteria and bacteria are all around us. What we should aim for is a clean, sweet-smelling place to live, where potentially hazardous bacteria are controlled by basic hygiene. A healthy human immune system can easily cope with normal household germs and is in fact at greater risk from the chemicals in many cleaning products.

Recent years have seen a boom in germicidal products, from kitchen sponges to plastic teething toys. Not only can germicides be health risks in themselves, but many disinfectants contain chemicals which can affect the central nervous system and cause organ damage.

Health and environmental experts caution against anti-microbial products (sponges, toys, soaps) because (1) they create a false sense of security (there is no evidence at all that they make a home safer); (2) they are likely to unfavourably alter the balance of microbial life in the home, leaving behind those that are harder to kill; (3) surviving bacteria are likely to become resistant, which could make homes, like hospitals, a harbour for truly dangerous microbacteria.

In a case where you truly need a stronger disinfectant, the best choice is a properly dilute solution of chlorine bleach. For general purposes, there are excellent natural disinfectants which include borax, tea tree oil, grapefruit seed oil and other citrus extracts. You'll find these in commercial products and can add them to solutions you make up.

The Cleaning Cupboard

Household products are designed to clean, disinfect and deodorise, but we often buy a promise rather than a truly superior product, and end up with a cupboard full of luridly-coloured plastic bottles. The following basic supplies will get you through every domestic task. They are unscented, but you can add a few drops of essential oil to create your own fresh and naturally clean smell. Look for containers which can be reused to conveniently package your basic cleaning supplies. Shakers are useful for bicarbonate of soda and borax, and spray bottles are good for a window-cleaning mixture. In a hard water area, add a little water softener to your cleaning bucket – that way, you'll need less detergent.

A Basic List

- *Cleaning cloths:* Cotton is best for cleaning and polishing, and linen is good for glass. Rags do not disintegrate or leave bits of fibre, and you can easily make them from old towels or T-shirts. Keep a plentiful supply in the kitchen, too. I soak used rags in a covered pail (an old nappy bucket) with water and a little borax, and launder weekly.
- *Apron with pockets:* A time-saver because you have somewhere to keep spare cloths, a spray bottle and scraper. And your clothes will stay clean.
- *Washing up liquid:* I use Ecover brand, but there are many others.
- *All-purpose cleaner:* I like the Ecover spray cleaner, but any basic detergent diluted in water may be what you need. Washing soda makes a potent cleaner for floors.
- *Abrasive powdered cleaner:* If you use a standard brand, get

one that is unscented and contains no chlorine. I use this for the toilet, with a firm brush.

- *Bicarbonate of soda:* Buy a 500g box from the chemist rather than the tiny ones you get for baking (one reader wrote that she'd like to buy it without being suspected of crack dealing!) It is a partial water softener.

- *White distilled vinegar:* Good for cleaning windows and tiles, descaling a kettle or removing stains from a teapot. Mixed with bicarbonate of soda, it will polish brass and copper.

- *Washing soda:* An alkaline water softener that will improve washing results and enable you to cut down on the amount of powder you use. It also cuts grease.

- *Borax:* A natural mineral product that kills germs and mildew. Use it to soak nappies, whiten clothes, soften water and increase the effectiveness of plain soap. It is also good at keeping down mould and preventing odours.

- *Trisodium phosphate (TSP):* TSP is a powerful cleaner that rinses away without leaving a residue. It is available from paint shops. Buy it 'straight' rather than mixed with detergents and fragrance. It is a phosphate and has a harmful effect on water supplies, but chemically sensitive people find it useful as it gives off no fumes.

- *Furniture paste wax:* Avoid all aerosol polishes, especially those containing silicone. Experts prefer to dust with a soft cloth slightly dampened with water. Good furniture needs an occasional waxing, no more than once a year.

- *Metal polish:* Lemon juice or white vinegar mixed with bicarbonate of soda will polish brass articles and toothpaste can be used to polish delicate jewellery.

- *Toilet cleaner:* Natural commercial products are simply acids (like vinegar), while bleach oxidises toilet stains rather than removing them. The ring in your toilet comes from hard water (just the same as the limescale in the kettle) and can be tackled with a simple pumice bar, which is completely non-toxic, or bit of wet and dry paper. Use a borax or tea tree oil solution to disinfect *(see Natural Disinfectants above).*

- *Window cleaner:* Mix two tablespoons of white vinegar with two cups of water and a few drops of liquid soap. Or try 45 per cent water, 45 per cent rubbing alcohol and 10 per cent household ammonia for a more toxic but effective product.
- *Carpet cleaning:* Use a steam-cleaning machine with plain water. For gentle cleaning and deodorising, sprinkle the carpet with plain bicarbonate of soda. Leave for an hour or two, then vacuum.
- *Oven cleaning:* Avoid caustic oven cleaner by wiping up spills and spatters. Put a baking sheet under dishes likely to boil over. For non-toxic cleaning, use steel wool after thoroughly wetting the oven walls and allowing the dirt to soften.

>Soap and Detergent

Soap is made from a fat that has been 'saponfied' – chemically changed through the addition of an alkali. Soap has been made for at least 1,000 years, and its basic functions are to cut grease and loosen dirt so it can be rinsed away.

Detergents are of more recent origin. They lower the surface tension of water and allow it to loosen dirt. Detergents are not as likely to be biodegradable and those that contain phosphate have contributed to water pollution.

Soap is a much simpler product, but detergents are often more effective on modern surfaces. They tend to be easier to rinse away completely, without leaving a soap scum (which can be cut with an acid, such as vinegar). Use simple soaps when you can, but don't worry about using some detergent.

> ## TIPS: FOR CURTAINS
> - Choose curtains that can be washed in water, rather than dry cleaned, though if you have lined curtains made from fabrics that need special care, dry cleaning may be your only option – unless 'wet cleaning' *(see page 44)* has come to your town. Curtains can be shaken and aired outside, a much easier and cheaper option than full-scale cleaning.

Air Freshening

Some people live near factories which provide continuous background odour – a sensory pollutant – and the emissions from chemical plants and busy roads are dangerous. Most of us do not have such substantial problems to contend with, but we still want to improve the air we breathe at home.

Don't equate the smell of bleach or other harsh cleaners with freshness. Commercial air fresheners work by masking unpleasant odours, coating your nasal passages with an oily film, or numbing your sense of smell with a nerve-deadening agent. Try some eco-living ideas instead.

TIPS: FOR AIR FRESHENING

- Increase and improve ventilation. Open strategic windows for a daily airing to clear stale or offensive odours, as well as any toxic fumes which might build up. An extractor fan can help in the kitchen and bathroom.
- Empty your rubbish frequently and sprinkle a little borax or bicarbonate of soda in the bottom of the bin. (Once you start composting, your rubbish bin will stay dry and is very unlikely to smell.)
- Declare your home a no-smoking zone or establish a single room for smokers, one which can be aired easily.
- Don't overheat your home. Steady background heat together with specific sources of radiant heat reduces stuffiness.
- Use bowls of water to humidify the air.
- Grow spider plants (*Chlorophytum*), golden pothos (*Scindapsus aureus*) and other plants to reduce indoor toxins and improve air quality.
- Fill bowls (or your car's ashtray) with a mixture of whole cloves and cinnamon bark and other spices. (Buy spices in bulk at an Asian market.)

To make flowers perfect the floral industry uses more pesticides than any other agricultural business, as well as vast quantities of synthetic accessories, floral preservatives and non-native flowers. Encourage your florist to use locally grown flowers and simply constructed arrangements.

Household Pests

Insecticides are poisonous and should be avoided because of their environmental effects and effects on our health. You're unlikely to have a problem with pests if you pay extra attention to cleaning and tidying, and block their entrances. Food should be stored in airtight containers (glass jars are excellent). Take special care with cleaning. Don't leave crumbs, and empty wastebaskets frequently. Ants and flies are said to dislike mint, and eucalyptus, citrus, citronella and clove oils are also insect repellants.

9

House and Home

A home – however it is shaped and whatever it is made of – is the most enduring, and expensive, investment we make. It is also one of the most important environmental decisions we make.

Our dwellings are where we retire for rest and sustenance and safety, where major events of loving and grieving and rejoicing take place. Our sense of home depends on external features, in the garden or down the street, that make up our neighbourhood or village or parish or city block. While *Eco Living* is primarily about the way we live in our homes, this chapter gives some attention to where we live and aspects of 'liveability' that go beyond our four walls.

Think Globally, Act Locally

The rapid changes in transport and work patterns of the past few decades have had a devastating impact on community life. And aspects of the environment around us affect our health and well-being, for good or ill.

Rapid transportation and telecommunications have brought the world to our shops and television screens, but too much thinking globally can impoverish our sense of home, for a connection depends on the things that make one place different from another. The environmental and arts organisation Common Ground has a slogan for the green consumer: 'Resist the things that can be found anywhere.'

You can add features of local distinctiveness to your home by serving local foods and drinks, decorating with old maps and prints, and preserving landmarks around your home. Don't tidy up too much – let old things weather gracefully – and help to preserve old buildings, hedgerows, orchards, family businesses and winding lanes. Encourage the use of local stone, brick and wood, and cherish local dialects, family histories and traditional names.

>Promote Biodiversity

The sense of place can be enhanced by the unique biodiversity of the area. As well as being preserved, biological resources need to be used in sustainable ways and the benefits of biodiversity – new medicines, for example – must be shared equitably.

TIPS: FOR ENCOURAGING BIODIVERSITY

- Protect the habitat of endangered creatures and restore degraded areas.
- Respect and preserve the practices of indigenous communities.
- Monitor the development and use of all biotechnology products.
- Leave existing ecosystems and wild places alone, concentrating new buildings on land already disturbed.
- Provide wildlife spaces in gardens and neighbourhoods.
- Refuse to buy rainforest woods
- Choose woods from a variety of native European species: beech, birch, oak, pine.
- In your garden, plant old roses and open-pollinated (non-hybridised) seeds.
- Buy recycled paper to discourage single-crop forestry.
- Buy 'heritage' fruit and vegetables, and paper made from hemp or jute or water hyacinth.

>Local Agenda 21

Local Agenda 21 is a global action programme set in motion at the 1992 Rio Earth Summit. Its purpose is to counter the effects of environmental deterioration on a global level while applying the action on a local level. LA21's focus is sustainability, taking into account:

- respect for environmental quality and natural resources global as well as local issues
- thinking beyond our lifetime
- finding a fairer basis for people to share both natural and man-made resources
- working with others to find the best way forward

LA21 involves three groups of 'stakeholders', people with an investment in the outcome: grassroots groups and individuals, local organisations such as schools, and local authorities. These groups together set goals – such as restoring historic buildings, creating nature reserves and educating townspeople – for Local Agenda 21 compliance. For more information, contact your council, Friends of the Earth or the National Federation of Women's Institutes, which has developed a strong Agenda 21 programme *(see Resources)*.

Ecological Design

There is a growing movement amongst architects, landscape architects and industrial designers to consider the ecological implications of the buildings, parks and products they help to create. Green design includes planning ways to save trees, preserve streams, reduce pollution from the construction process and replant native species of trees, shrubs and wildflowers. Wetlands can be protected from sediment and runoff, and buildings can be designed around natural features and views.

Ecological design also includes an emphasis on vernacular design – that is, using the materials, colours, shapes and structures traditional or native to the area, rather than trying to imitate a Tuscan farmhouse in the fens of Cambridgeshire. Vernacular interior design makes sense. The cosy, rather cluttered effect of the traditional British home, replete with bright chintzes and wood surfaces, is just right in a damp, cool climate.

>Furniture

Good-quality second-hand furniture is often a far better buy than new storeroom items and for household items there are auctions and sale rooms, ranging from cheap and seedy to very exalted indeed.

Also, a reconditioned vacuum cleaner may give many more years of service than a bright new plastic one *(for more information on cleaning, see Chapter 8)*.

>Good Wood

The choices we make when we buy wood have huge environmental consequences. You may have bought one of the million doors imported into Britain from tropical countries each year without having the slightest idea that you were contributing to the destruction of the rainforests. Fortunately, Friends of the Earth has produced a *Good Wood Guide* to promote the use of sustainably-produced timber from Europe and North America and well-managed tropical forests and major British retailers have revamped their timber buying in co-operation with the World Wide Fund for Nature UK and the Forest Stewardship Council.

There are a variety of choices. 'Rediscovered wood' is the best – this is wood salvaged from demolished properties, urban tree salvage and even demolition landfills. You'll also see eco-furniture and picture frames made from obviously reused 'distressed' wood (complete with worn paint and nail holes). 'Green wood' includes formaldehyde-free composite panels, arsenic-free pressure-treated lumber, engineered structural wood products and even 'plastic lumber' made from recycled plastics. 'Certified wood' is produced to standards set by the Forest Stewardship Council with the aim of strengthening local economies and protecting ecosystems, water quality and wildlife habitats, and is stamped as FSG-certified.

British and European woods should be chosen in preference to tropical hardwoods such as iroko and mahogany because even if these are sustainably harvested, there are high-energy costs involved in transporting wood around the world.

>Timber Treatments

Serious health damage has been attributed to chemicals used for common timber treatments required by most building societies and indemnity insurers. Lawsuits have been brought against timber treatment firms by people whose homes were treated and former employees who now suffer from acute health problems.

While firms and government bodies are researching non-chemical ways of treating wood, products currently in use include lindane, TBTO and various pentachlorophenates. Lindane is a broad-spectrum organochloride insecticide and a known carcinogen. TBTO is an extremely dangerous chemical, now banned as an anti-foulant for boats and banned in many other countries for home wood treatment (German research suggests that it causes psychosis, anxiety and other central nervous system disorders).

Some commercial timber treatment firms will, if requested, use non-chemical methods to treat fungal decay by cutting out all rotten timber, removing sources of damp and then carefully monitoring moisture levels. Permethrin is a less toxic alternative developed for use in buildings where there are bats. Another alternative is inorganic boron. Heat treatment can be used to treat woodworm in small pieces of furniture and in Denmark it is used to kill dry rot. Careful design and maintenance can eliminate the need for rot treatment. If you are buying a home, contact the London Hazards Centre or the Ecological Design Association for further information.

>Daylighting

Modern buildings are designed on the principle that artificial lighting is just as good as, perhaps better than, natural daylight, but the newest thinking on building design – especially for schools and office buildings used only during the day – is that daylighting is an essential design component, increasing worker productivity and improving student performance.

The solution to the apparent conflict between human health needs for sufficient natural full-spectrum light and the environmentalists' contention that we should use energy-saving fluorescent bulbs is to use artificial lighting more carefully and increase the amount of natural light we use in our homes and offices.

Here are some design principles to keep in mind when you arrange rooms and lighting. In addition to improving the light quality indoors, these also reduce energy consumption.

TIPS: FOR LIGHTING

- Choose a southerly exposure.
- Arrange rooms by the availability and timing of daylight. Rooms you use in the morning should face east, and those used in the afternoon and evening should face west. Dark rooms, facing north or a blank brick wall, or with no windows, should be used least.
- Prune or move trees and shrubs that limit the light your house receives.
- Deciduous trees can be used to block hot summer sun, while allowing low winter sun to enter the house.
- Curtains should pull entirely off the window on a long track or rail. Make sure that blinds roll completely off the window.

- Clean windows let in more light (and clean light bulbs produce more light).
- Skylights are excellent for illuminating hallways and stairs. If you are making alterations in your house, think about placing small interior windows to maximise lighting where it is most needed.

>Moving House

Things to look for when you move:

- local schools, shops, libraries, parks and other facilities
- diversified public transportation (buses, trains, vans, foot and cycle paths)
- progressive environmental policies and services *(see Resources to send for the model environmental services charter drawn up by the Department of the Environment and the Regions)*
- active citizens' groups
- available local health care

Choose the smallest home you can. Big houses use more energy and materials to build or maintain and housing developments are, along with roads, the major cause of species loss. Only 55 per cent of new homes are built on previously developed land.

Ecological Renovation

All houses need regular maintenance and as old buildings are turned to new uses renovation is increasingly common. Renovating an existing building is less damaging to the environment than building a new one and there are many ways to reduce the impact of renovation while creating a healthier and more beautiful home. Most importantly, renovations can make our homes more energy-efficient.

TIPS: FOR RENOVATION

- Salvage as much as possible for reuse. Contractors don't like to do this because it takes longer, but maybe you can handle certain stages of the demolition yourself.
- Call your local council environmental health officer to find out what materials can be recycled in your area. They may be able to refer you to a charity that will welcome some of your discards.
- Beware of hazards in the materials you remove: lead paint, lead solder, asbestos and wood treated with long-lasting pesticides. Never burn any hazardous material.
- Use the least-toxic methods as you work, choosing hand tools and scraping surfaces by hand rather than using chemicals, if possible. A steam cleaner is a great eco-renovation tool which uses no chemicals at all to effectively remove distemper (limewash) or old wallpaper, and you can use it instead of chemical degreasers too.
- Replace inefficient older windows, if your budget allows, with new high-performance thermally efficient windows. Most of these work through a combination of double- or triple-paned glass and tight sealing. This is a long-term energy saving investment, considerably less expensive and more attractive than double glazing. This is also a good time to improve wall and loft insulation.
- Finally, complete the cycle by choosing new building products made from recycled materials. These include certain insulation materials, composites used for countertops and even recycled paint.

>Preferred Materials

- *Insulation:* cellulose, perlite; vermiculite; fibreglass, rock wool; cork
- *Weatherstripping:* metal
- *Interior walls and ceilings:* gypsum board or plaster
- *Caulking:* linseed oil putty; clear silicone
- *Flooring:* brick, slate, untreated wood, concrete, ceramic tile; natural linoleum; untreated natural fibre carpets; architectural salvage
- *Cabinetry:* solid sustainably harvested wood; enamelled metal; architectural salvage

- *Countertops:* ceramic tile; wood; granite; marble; architectural salvage
- *Plumbing:* copper pipes with lead-free solder or mechanical joints

>Paints and Finishes

Paints, varnishes and the various solvents we use to mix them and to clean up afterwards can be dangerous and also present disposal problems. This is why the odour of new paint gives many people headaches.

One of the things prospective parents always do is paint the nursery to make it look bright and pristine. They don't realise that paint can pollute the air. While all-natural paints are much more expensive than ordinary commercial brands, they should definitely be used in infants' and children's rooms. You'll be pleased by their light, slightly aromatic scent. As an intermediate step, choose water-based products and improve ventilation. Fresh air is more effective than heat in drying paint. If possible, allow a room to dry for several days before you move into it. Paint the baby's room well in advance of the birth. Another option is to make your own paints. These include traditional water-based distemper and milk paint.

The most natural furniture finish is simple oil or wax, and traditional shellac is made from natural materials, not petro-chemical products. While you'll need to turn to a specialist publication for advice on applying these finishes, it is reassuring to note that the alternatives to polyurethane are relatively cheap and durable, as well as very attractive.

>Fabrics and Furnishings

Environmental toxins come from furniture, floor coverings and other domestic fittings. People who are chemically sensitive can have extreme reactions – burning feelings in the lungs, rashes and headaches – and there have been many cases of so-called 'sick building syndrome' after the installation of new carpets, which are treated with a range of chemicals to make them stain-resistant and moth repellant and to make them look and feel more luxurious.

The resins used to bind plywood and chipboard and to treat furnishing fabrics are significant sources of formaldehyde vapour, which is highly irritating to some people and may cause allergic reactions in children. Formaldehyde is particularly hazardous because it seems to act as a trigger for acute chemical sensitivity. Studies have found that the concentration of formaldehyde vapour in the air tripled after chipboard furniture was installed in an otherwise empty house.

Cotton and wool futons provide excellent bedding for sensitive individuals, and latex foam and feathers are good choices for pillows and cushions.

Your nose is a good guide to some chemical air pollution. If a new shower curtain has a distinctive plastic smell, it is outgassing chemicals. The odour of a new rug or carpet can be removed by steam cleaning with plain water after installation. Certain smells disappear quickly and you can speed the outgassing process by improving ventilation. Have new carpets fitted in the summer when you can leave windows open, choose solid wood furniture and don't replace old chipboard if possible.

DIY Products

Many of these contain hydrocarbon solvents, which are so toxic that they can cause death by inhalation. Take great care when using them, use as little as possible and choose alternative products when you can.

TIPS: FOR DIY

- Buy only what you absolutely need and cannot find a substitute for.
- Work outside if possible and try not to breathe fumes.
- Put the lid back on when using any volatile chemical – nail polish remover, paint thinner – so the liquid in the container doesn't vaporise into the air you're breathing.
- Never mix products unless the label says you can.
- Wear protective clothing and a mask if necessary, and protect your hands with rubber gloves.
- Avoid wearing soft contact lenses while working with any solvent.
- Store products in the original container.
- Use up what you've bought or take leftovers to a hazardous waste collection point. If that's not possible, place them, carefully sealed and wrapped, in the dustbin – not down the drain!

10

Your Green Garden

What bothers me most about *Star Wars* movies is that there are no plants, nothing green, nothing alive except humans and various weird-looking aliens. Plants are the foundation of our ability to live on Earth and a seed is miraculous, a microcosm of life. Gardening provides an escape into the natural world, a connection with the Earth itself in all its lush wild messiness.

In a garden, shrubs and flowers disguise unattractive features, offer privacy, shelter and food for wildlife and generally beautify our surroundings. Even a small garden can offer quite a good supply of flowers and greenery for the house. Plant plenty of bulbs to brighten your springtime and provide cutting flowers too (make sure they are commercially grown, not wild harvested).

Experts say it is possible to grow enough vegetables for one person's annual consumption on a 10'x10' plot of land, the size of a small bedroom. Double that area and you can also grow a year's supply of soft fruit. After the initial hard work, 5–10 minutes a day should maintain that 100 square feet. Novice gardeners on neglected city soil can't expect those yields, but many domestic gardens have a plot this big which could be devoted to vegetable growing.

Green thumbs can be cultivated. They depend on a combination of knowledge, instinct and keen observation, tuning in to the rhythms and signals of the natural world, and perhaps for this reason many people suffering from stress find gardening particularly satisfying.

Permaculture

Permaculture (permanent agriculture) is an ecological design system or philosophy, and for some people it's become a philosophy for life. The basis of permaculture is using Nature as a model for doing things, from growing food to building houses, with a goal of minimising impact on the environment. A practical application is to include food-bearing and other useful perennials in your garden – raspberries, nuts, mushrooms, willow and poplar, for example. When you put in trees and shrubs, consider varieties which will offer crops as a bonus. Fruit trees, grapevines and quince bushes (which have lovely pink and white flowers and sulphur-coloured fruit which is excellent in pies and jam) are favourites. Why not let the brambles grow at the bottom of the garden and give them a little manure in the spring? (You might prefer to plant cultivated blackberry varieties to get a higher yield.) Tuck herbs in amongst your flowers, in beds and in windowboxes. Try to keep some parsley, mint and other favourite herbs near the kitchen; you won't use them half as often if you have to trek to the other end of the back garden.

TIPS: FOR GARDENING
- Garden with someone else if you can.
- Take it easy. When you are digging, make sure your tool handles are long enough, bend your knees and not your back, turn to throw the spadeful of soil after you have straightened up – and don't try to do the whole patch in one afternoon.
- Wear gloves and a hat and/or sun screen to protect your neck, face and nose.
- Pay for some help if you have a lot of space to tackle – or exchange...

- Buy or borrow the best tools you can afford — they will make physical labour a pleasure.
- Don't overspend — new gardeners tend to go a little mad buying equipment and seeds.
- Join the Organic Horticultural Association (OHA) (*see Resources*) for practical advice on organic gardening.
- Watch TV gardening programmes and borrow books from the library. Many newspaper gardening columns are excellent, too.
- Admire your neighbours' gardens: if you're lucky you'll get tips on dealing with your area's quirks of sun or soil.
- Visit gardens open to the public through the National Gardens Scheme or the OHA-run demonstration organic garden near Coventry.
- Share an allotment with a friend. You can cover each other over holidays and provide moral support during bad weather. The closer your allotment is to your home, the more often you will visit it.

Soil Testing

It is useful to know the composition of your soil, so that you can choose plants that will grow well there. The home test kits available at nurseries will tell you about pH, nitrogen, phosphate and potash levels, but some town and city soil is badly contaminated with lead, so you may need to have your soil tested before you start growing edible plants, for example. Some councils now regularly test allotments and you can get advice from the Organic Horticultural Association about having your soil professionally tested for chemical contamination.

Choosing Plants and Seeds

>Biodiversity

Current UK legislation has virtually eliminated many old varieties by establishing a list of 'approved' seeds. Plant varieties can be patented and royalties collected on seed sales. Unfortunately, the process of getting a seed variety onto the list and keeping it there is expensive and every year more seed varieties are lost. This is a disaster on three counts: (1) large firms with agrochemical ties, such as ICI, are profiting at the expense of smaller, family-run seed companies; (2) the hybrids which are sold to commercial growers are flavourless varieties which require large inputs of chemical fertilisers and pesticides (so our environment is polluted and we get tasteless and less nutritious food in the bargain); (3) genetic variety is being lost.

Lawrence Hills of the Organic Horticulture Association (OHA) helped Oxfam to found the world's first vegetable gene bank to preserve the hundreds of British varieties which it has become illegal to sell. Join the OHA and get their advice on how to buy seeds from small firms which are campaigning to have this legislation changed.

Q Grow plants from seed to get stronger, organically grown seedlings with a far greater choice of variety.

Feeding the Soil

'Compost', like 'organic', has more than one meaning. There is the potting mixture which you buy to fill a windowbox and, vital to the organic gardener, there is the compost which you make yourself from whatever organic materials you have to hand.

The simplest approach is to mark an area about four feet square, loosen up the soil with a fork and pile on a layer of twigs to keep the bottom aerated, then add whatever you've got whenever it comes along. Sides can be built of scrap timber and in wet weather it should be covered with a piece of old carpet. Layer kitchen scraps, grass clippings, leaves, plant clippings –

anything made of natural materials (I actually throw old jeans and jumpers into mine).

Compost needs to be 'activated' with something high in nitrogen. Fresh manure and seaweed work well, comfrey and nettles are both useful, but an even easier and readily available activator is urine – in olden days it was called 'liquid gold'.

The annual burning of leaves wastes a wonderful resource. Leaf mould is richer in minerals than peat moss, available locally and better to use because the 'mining' of bog peat is destroying important habitat. Making leaf mould is dead easy: just pile or bag the leaves and wait for a year or two until they break down.

A simple way to add nutrients to the soil, smother weeds and cut down on the watering you need to do is to use a mulch. This is a thick layer (you should not be able to see the soil) of some organic material like straw, leafmould or homemade garden compost. A layer of newspaper will help to eradicate perennial weeds.

As for manure, horse manure from your local stables will contain residues of chemicals from the horses' feed and from worming products. Home gardeners can have ready-to-use manure, garden and potting compost from Soil Association standard organic farms delivered anywhere in the country (contact the Soil Association for further details; see Resources).

Paving

York stone makes the best paved surface, but quarrying and hauling stone around the country are not desirable. The best option is to find local stone or to buy used paving or old bricks. Concrete or asphalt blocks natural drainage, affects the microclimate and does nothing useful with the solar energy which falls on it.

Make a surface or path with old bricks or paving stones, set in dirt so that mosses and plants can grow between the cracks and the delicate ecology of earthworms, plant and insect life will be preserved.

TIPS: FOR EASIER MODERN GARDENING

- Don't grow houseplants – they're far more work than outdoor plants.
- Dig your garden near the house to make it easier to pick food for meals. Mix flowers and vegetables and herbs and fruit for a truly modern garden.
- Tackle a small area at a time.
- Choose pest-resistant varieties adapted to your climate and garden conditions.
- Grow things you love to eat or smell.
- Plant perennials or self-sowing annuals.
- Use easy techniques such as mulching and no-dig beds.
- Live and let live: gardening should be fun, not a military campaign.

Pest Control

Keeping pests under control without using dangerous chemicals is not the hurdle you might think. Stronger plants are more disease-resistant and organic gardeners make use of companion planting and natural predators like ladybirds. There are a number of sprays and powders available, including the plant-derived pesticides derris and pyrethrum. These biological controls can be supplemented with mechanical controls (sticky traps and removing beetles by hand), and carefully choosing plants that are pest resistant. Companion planting is another organic technique: you can plant mint, which most insects dislike, near plants more attractive to pests.

Slugs and snails are probably the worst problem for the organic gardener. Chemical slug pellets are a well-known danger to birds, which sometimes eat the dead slugs, and they kill natural aphid predators too. Eco techniques to deal with slugs range from saucers of beer and upended grapefruit shells to night hunts with a torch and a bucket of soapy water.

You can also reduce pests in the garden by eliminating standing water.

>Dealing with Insects

Insects can spoil the great outdoors for many of us, but many products to repel them are ferocious poisons. On the other hand, non-toxic herbal repellants often don't work terribly well. False labelling is common – I've seen a typical chemical product labelled 'eco-spray'.

Rather than apply commercial repellants, which contain Deet (diethyl toluamide), a strong irritant which can eat through plastic and dissolve paint, rub your skin with vinegar (on a cotton wool ball) and allow it to dry. The smell disappears as it dries, but makes you taste nasty. An alternative is to rub on oil of citronella or pennyroyal, diluted in a little vegetable oil. Citronella candles are standard insect repellants in the United States.

Don't overrate the problem. A few gnats do not merit an assault with dangerous chemicals. Don't apply repellants until you are sure they are necessary – these products should never become routine (unlike hats and sun block lotions). Learn to live with the occasional fly or mosquito. When insects are really fierce, stay out of their way. No repellant can deal with hordes of blackfly.

Look for new products like 'bug-buttons' that keep repellants off your skin and apply products to your skin only when all other means fail.

Paraphenalia

The average garden centre is full of plastic equipment and tools, plastic pots and polystyrene trays, but try to stick to biodegradable materials.

Old newspapers, for example, can be used to make a homemade version of peat pots. Wrap six or eight sheets around a bottle to form a cylinder and fasten with an 'organic' glue like Gloy. When dry, cut into suitable lengths, place the rings of newspaper in a large garden tray and fill with potting soil. The whole thing can be planted in the garden. Choose a biodegradable, untreated gardening string or use strips of cloth to tie up your tomatoes. After harvesting, both plants and ties can go straight onto the compost pile.

❓ Yoghurt tubs and plastic packing trays are useful for planting seeds in and you can cut the bottom off plastic mineral water bottles to make mini-cloches.

TIPS: FOR WATER CONSERVATION

- Save rainwater in a barrel or water butt and use it on the garden or to wash the car – or bicycle. Cover to make it safe – and to prevent mosquitoes breeding.
- Plant species which don't need masses of water. Xeriscape is a way of planting with native and similar species that need no additional water at all – a great timesaver.
- Apply thick mulches to cut watering to a minimum.
- Water early in the morning or at dusk, so the water doesn't just evaporate.
- Use soaker hoses rather than sprinklers.

Trees

The loss of forests, both temperate and tropical, is one of this century's greatest disasters. Trees have a special place in human consciousness – in Jungian psychology they stand for wholeness. They are vital to our sense of place. A mighty oak or ash, or an orchard of apple and pear trees, is one of the beauties of town or countryside. Trees also perform vital functions, improving air quality, creating habitats for birds and insects, and cooling streets and buildings.

In spite of our love of trees and our concern about the rainforests, however, England today has only 7 per cent tree cover. In the EU, only Ireland has fewer trees and the Countryside Commission has urged the government to make every effort to increase the amount of land set aside for tree planting.

Existing trees are under threat. Cable television is creating a new environmental problem, as more than 100 cable franchises licensed by the Department of Trade and Industry lay cables along an estimated 50 miles of streets each day. The damage is not immediately visible, but tree roots are severed or damaged in the process, and thousands of trees are dying a lingering death.

Urban trees need people as much as people need them. They should be planted where they provide not just attractive greenery but also shade during hot spells, a pleasant spot for a seat or a good place for children to play, because this means that the people who enjoy them will also care for them.

Gardening for Wildlife

Encourage wildlife in your garden – domestic gardens can provide an extra habitat for beleaguered creatures whose natural habitats are being chewed up by development, and birds and toads will eat insect pests.

Eco Living

TIPS: FOR ATTRACTING WILDLIFE

- Set up a bird table or hang a feeder. Put it somewhere where you can see it from the house, but out of reach of cats.
- Plant native trees and shrubs which support a wide range of insect life. This in turn attracts birds, hedgehogs, frogs and toads – an ecological cycle in the making!
- Hedges provide a home for many creatures. You can prune trees such as field maple and hawthorn into an excellent thick hedge or windbreak.
- Plant native wildflowers – snowdrops, bluebells, violets and primroses, poppies, cornflowers and oxeye daisies.
- Plant a wildflower lawn.
- Plant old-fashioned sweet-scented cottage flowers to attract bees and butterflies and birds.
- Leave the weeds. This can easily get out of hand, but try setting aside one area for nettles, wild parsley and buttercups.
- Build a pond. Habitat for frogs and toads is declining in the countryside, so friendly gardens are important for their survival.

TIPS: FOR AN ORGANIC LAWN

- Choose an appropriate seed blend. A hard-wearing mixture will be easier to maintain (and the weeds won't be quite so obvious).
- Minimise the lawn area. All most of us want is a pleasant stretch of green and the smaller the area you have to maintain, the easier it will be to use organic methods.
- Allow extra lawn space to go wild, or plant a wildflower lawn, or another ground cover.
- Set your (non-electric) mower blades to two inches. Lawns do best if cut fairly high, but frequently.
- Leave lawn clippings where they fall, to replenish the soil.
- Remember that worms are good for the soil. Sweep the castings around on a dry day.
- Spike the lawn, either with a fork or with spiked boots (available from gardening shops).
- Feed it with a high-nitrogen natural fertiliser two or three times a year. Seaweed meal is very good and so is sifted compost.
- Arm yourself with an old kitchen knife to dig out dandelions and dock – or you can leave the dandelions, eat the early sprouts in a salad and make the flowers into wine.

Outdoor Living

Make the garden an outdoor room, with a table, chairs, play equipment and shelves, and an accessible storage area. Provide sheltered seats in sunny spots and create privacy with climbing plants on a trellis or on wires. White flowers show up at dusk and after dark, so if you are going to use your garden then it is worth concentrating on white blooms. Some form of lighting will make the garden more enticing on mild evenings.

11

Getting Around

We're all on the move these days, and more and more often by car. We've become accustomed to the speed and convenience of driving, and we're somehow oblivious to its inconveniences and many negative effects. Car ownership is considered, around the world, the most important sign of affluence. But because transport contributes a third of the carbon dioxide that causes global warming, many experts believe the single greatest environmental challenge is to rethink the way we get around, and to change our attitude towards cars.

This chapter looks at what's wrong with our dependence on the car, at ways to reduce driving and improve health, and then at prospects for healthy mixed transportation and neighbourhoods that are not dependent on cars. (*Air travel is discussed in Chapter 14.*)

Q A single gallon of petrol produces 5½lb of carbon dioxide!

Shopping centres are increasingly taking shopping away from neighbourhoods and villages into centralised sites which are geared to car owners – in spite of the fact that in the US, where this trend started, 20 per cent of the malls standing in 1990 have closed. People are now looking for places where they can shop and dine – and often live too – without using a car. Traditional

US main streets are being revitalised and neo-traditional developers are building 'new urban' communities and shopping areas, sometimes on the site of old malls.

In the UK, 99 per cent of the national transport budget is devoted to the automobile and traffic is expected to increase by 20–40 per cent over the next decade. Driving is encouraged through the neglect of public transport, through road building and tax concessions.

Cars and Health

Car engines are a major cause of air pollution, emitting nitrogen oxide, carbon monoxide, benzene, hydrocarbons and sulphur dioxide as well as lead. These emissions cause headaches and smarting eyes and throat, and long-term damage including respiratory problems from bronchitis and asthma to leukaemia and lung cancer. The annual global health cost of air pollution is estimated at some £13 billion.

Equally important to our health is the fact that driving requires no physical effort. Some of us make up for this with regular exercise, but many people do not. Cutting down on car use could substantially improve human health through increased exercise.

Traffic congestion and noise are also considerable sources of modern stress. Many people will go to almost any length to avoid traffic jams and there are increasing numbers of so-called 'road rage' incidents, in which people become violent towards other drivers and pedestrians.

Traffic noise is an insidious pollutant, perhaps most striking in its absence – when, for example, snow blocks the roads. Many people hesitate to open windows because of the roar of traffic outside their homes, while others have trouble getting to sleep at night because of cars and motorcycles zooming past.

Cars and the Community

Cars are inherently dangerous: they are large, heavy objects which travel at high speeds in close proximity to pedestrians and cyclists. They take up large amounts of space – as much as one third the land area of a town – and dominate our physical space. They have dramatically curtailed children's freedom to roam, making them less fit and less independent.

Researchers increasingly find that when shops, schools, workplaces and homes are separated by long distances, people meet only in well-defined and impersonal indoor spaces, not in the casual and frequent situations that make us feel connected. This is an important aspect of the modern sense of alienation and a reason for the surging interest in neo-traditional housing developments in the US.

Cars and the Natural World

The less contact we have with a place, the less we care about it. If you always step out of your door into a car, you may not know the trees that grow along your own street. When you read that the countryside is under threat, it won't mean much to you from the front seat of a car speeding down the M3. Motorways cut swathes through large stretches of the country, obliterating everything in their path. We city-dwellers can be extraordinarily insensitive to the consequences of our demands on even nearby stretches of countryside and let our convenience overshadow the destructive impact of more roads on the villages and towns *en route* to our destinations.

Many valuable and beautiful wildlife sites have been destroyed and more are on the chopping block. Roads also have a disastrous effect on animals. A sheet of hard exposed surface, with continually moving high-speed metal objects, poses an insurmountable barrier for them. Noise drives them away and toxic fumes pollute their food and water. Roads are considered a major threat to biodiversity and they are changing the character of the towns and villages that are an essential part of the British landscape.

Travel Stress

>Driving Less

For most of us, driving isn't all or nothing. We can make choices, balancing our concern about the environment against the practical demands of our lives. Some areas have infrequent or inconvenient public transport and safety is often an issue for women. But maintaining a car is time-consuming and expensive. Taking taxis occasionally and hiring a car a couple of times a year works out considerably cheaper than keeping your own vehicle, while walking to the bus stop or the station might provide enough exercise to keep you in reasonable shape.

TIPS: FOR DRIVING LESS AND SAVING ENERGY

- Choose to live where you won't have to drive a lot.
- Live near where you work, work at home or talk to your company about telecommuting.
- Consciously plan ways to reduce travel: buy in bulk (which is convenient and saves money too) and run many errands on one trip.
- Don't drive alone. Try car-pooling to work if you cannot use public transport, share driving the children to school and do your weekly shopping with a friend.
- Tune up your bike and start wearing comfortable walking shoes.

- Try not to use the car for short journeys – catalytic converters don't work until they're warmed up.
- Think twice before purchasing another car.
- Choose a fuel-efficient car.
- Buy a second-hand car. Major problems show themselves in the first 20,000 miles, so a second-hand car is often a better bet than a new one – and of course they are much cheaper.
- Do not choose a diesel engine, because they produce far more particulant pollution than standard engines.
- Slow down to save petrol. Consumption is highest in start-and-stop town traffic and at over 55 mph on the motorway.
- Be ready to switch to greener fuels (natural gas, methane, ethanol).
- Drive with control and patience. Aggressive driving uses 20 per cent more petrol. Avoid slamming on the brakes, use the gears to slow down and don't rev the engine.
- Keep your car regularly tuned and the tyres fully inflated.
- Ensure that your car's oil and batteries are recycled.
- Remove roof racks when not in use and empty out the boot.
- Use asbestos-free brake pads and radial tyres.
- Join the Environmental Transport Association instead of the AA or RAC *(see Resources)*.

>Improving Traffic

Traffic patterns and car parking are some of the most important factors in creating liveable communities. Here are six principles to keep in mind if you are trying to improve the traffic situation in your town or neighbourhood:

- Improve public transportation and increase public awareness of the benefits of using it.
- Install special cycling facilities: exempt cyclists from some one-way restrictions and road closures as well as providing special cycle paths and turning lanes.
- Demand wider and higher pavements to increase pedestrians' security, traffic humps and frequent pedestrian crossings. Well-

lit footpaths and pedestrian shopping areas also encourage people to leave the car at home.

- Make residential streets unattractive to rat-running motorists by adjusting traffic priorities at junctions and installing road closures and chicanes.
- Reduce vehicle speeds with traffic humps and width restrictions.
- Encourage the local authority, and homeowners, to plant trees and shrubs, which muffle noise, improve the air and can make streets far more pleasant for residents.

Better Ways to Get Around

There's no single solution to our transportation needs. The first consideration for town planners (and government officials) should be accessibility, not mobility per se. We want to be able to get to and do certain things. One rule of thumb is that we should use a car only for distances over two miles – and of course, ecologically, we should try to live where many things we need are available within that two-mile radius. The evolution of global communications makes it possible to reduce travel to some extent, and by adopting a 'mixed transport' strategy for yourself or your household – using public transport, walking, cycling and driving when you must – you can keep tonnes of CO_2 out of the atmosphere.

Some people are so used to driving everywhere they think they'll melt if a raindrop falls on them. On the contrary, being outside – in rain, in wind, even in snow – is good for us. Our bodies are designed to cope gracefully with most weather and it's invigorating to experience the seasons: snowflakes on the tongue, raindrops curling your hair. Seasonal temperature changes are good for your immune system, so don't think you have to hide indoors, especially when there is wonderful high-tech sports gear available that works well for cyclist commuters or all-season runners.

>Public Transport

Both city and country dwellers need more reliable, faster, cleaner, safer and more comprehensive bus and train services. The closure of rural bus routes and train lines has left people in many villages and country areas isolated, or increasingly dependent on cars. But people won't turn *en masse* to public transportation until the government puts money into improving services. Government expenditure on public transport is called a 'subsidy', while money spent on more and bigger roads is not. Unfortunately, recent government initiatives to encourage the use of public transport may be undone by concerns about rail safety – a reason to insist on topnotch equipment and careful regulation.

We should support public transport, both with our votes and by using it whenever we can. Join public pressure groups like Sustrans, Transport 2000 and Friends of the Earth, as well as local associations which campaign on traffic issues. (Ironically, the best way to speed up car travel is to improve public transport.)

Think about the personal benefits to not driving: you have time to read, doze or meditate, or eavesdrop, with no worries about parking or about having a drink. But public transport requires different planning to car travel:

- Assemble a complete collection of timetables and maps for your area, or bookmark websites that will help you plan local and longer trips.
- Prominently note the information numbers for services you use often.
- Take time to enquire about reduced price fares or cards.
- Note the times of last buses, trains and night buses – and the number of a reliable minicab service won't go amiss either.

- Ask about working on flexi-time – this makes it possible to travel off-peak.

>Walking

Walking is a way to get around but it is also a vital pleasure, the best way to recharge and refresh your spirit, and an ideal background for concentrated – or idle – thought. On foot, you notice the first tinge of autumn colour in the trees and enjoy the scent of newly turned earth or a luxurious bank of honeysuckle. When I first went to work in London, I spent every lunch hour walking (sadly, today cars are far more intrusive, the air more polluted).

The health benefits of walking include fresh air and natural light. No special gear is required, but a small rucksack can be more comfortable than carrying a handbag. Put your high heels in it and change when you get to your destination. (*For more about walking, see Chapter 5.*)

>On your Bike

Cycling is a convenient, efficient and enjoyable way to get around. It's much faster than walking, faster than driving in many cities and eminently suited to short journeys.

In spite of the inevitable frustrations caused by sharing the road with cars, cycling is an important part of mixed transportation. World-wide, bicycles outnumber cars two to one. The bicycle is a vehicle for people of all ages – sometimes called the 'vehicle for a small planet'.

Britain, however, lags behind other European countries in cycle-friendliness. In Denmark, ten times as many journeys are made by bicycle than in Britain (20 per cent compared to our 2 per cent); in Amsterdam, where the climate is no better than ours, a third of journeys are made by bicycle. In Groningen, 57 per cent of the population travels by bicycle.

The more people cycle, the safer all cyclists will be. We need separate bicycle paths, plenty of marked bicycle routes and counter-flow lanes on one-way streets. Sustrans National Cycle Network has almost 5,000 miles of cycle paths all over Britain and aims to have 9,000 miles by 2005.

If you want to start bicycling but feel nervous, stick to local journeys and quiet streets until you develop the skills and confidence to cope with traffic. Bicyclists can be far more flexible than drivers, using quieter residential roads to make travelling less stressful, safer and faster. Friends of the Earth can put you in touch with a local cycling group, many of which produce maps to share advice on good routes and cycle paths.

Many people wonder whether the benefits of bicycling are not outweighed by the exhaust fumes. Some cyclists choose to wear masks to avoid breathing in smoke particulates, while others simply try to avoid heavy traffic. In any case, studies have found that the benefits of exercise outweigh the exposure to fumes – in fact, the air inside a car in heavy traffic is often more polluted than the air outside.

Children and Bikes

A quarter of the car journeys made by families with children under the age of fifteen are escort journeys – to and from school, sports activities, music lessons or friends' houses. It's no surprise that our children don't get enough exercise.

Cycling is an ideal way for older children and teenagers to get around and Transport 2000 has been working with schools to develop programmes that will get kids on their bikes. These innovative programmes focus on the benefits of walking and cycling: connection with the place where you live, physical fitness, self-confidence and independence. Cycling is also a great way to develop physical co-ordination.

Help your child work out cycle routes and take trips together. You can even carry a young child on your bike, with a child seat and child-size helmet. Some parents use a tricycle or a trailer seat, which is very practical for shopping.

TIPS: FOR YOUR BICYCLE

- Buy a second-hand bike. You don't need an ultralight racer or mountain bike for commuting or shopping.
- Make sure the seat is at the right height and comfortable (women may want to buy a seat made to fit a wider pelvis).
- Wear a helmet, plenty of reflective gear and bands for your trouser legs.
- A bell is a great safety device.
- Attach a big basket to make it easy to carry things.
- Wear a pair of old trainers – office shoes can be chewed up by bicycle pedals and toe clips – and carry an extra shirt in warm weather or if you're inclined to imagine yourself in the Tour de France.

Transport of the Future

The benefits of a mixed green transport system will include an increased sense of community, thriving small businesses, safer food (grown and produced closer to home) and lively towns and neighbourhoods, thanks to a greater mix of residential and commercial activities.

Nothing will alter the negative social effects of cars or make them take up less space. But we are not going to return to a car-less society. We therefore need super efficiency with new materials, direct-hydrogen fuel cells, integrated whole-system engineering – cars with innovations that go far beyond today's 'green' cars.

There are designs and technology already in development that will make cars safe, roomy and competitively priced, that will produce a car that, says US energy guru Amory Lovins, 'emits nothing but hot drinking water, doesn't rust or dent or fatigue, performs like a sports car, and gets 110 mpg'. Such vehicles will do away with two-thirds of the carbon problem caused by current models. Serious efforts are underway to get these cars on the market and you can help by buying them when they come out or investing in them now. *(See http://www.hypercarcenter.org for details.)* The next step will be to make them a global standard. In the meantime, an overall reduction in driving is the single best step to protecting our climate, safeguarding our health and making the world better for today's and tomorrow's children.

(12)
The Green Workplace

You can make your home environment healthier, but unless you take steps to create a greener office you may still suffer from the effects of ozone pollution (from photocopiers and printers) and a stiff neck from a poorly positioned computer screen. Offices and other workplaces deserve special attention because we spend so much of our time in them. And businesses use a lot of natural resources and create considerable waste – the average office worker uses 10–20lb of paper each month. Whatever changes you can get your company to make will probably do more for the environment than similar changes at home – so make the effort!

Many of the health topics discussed in other chapters are relevant to businesses and workplaces, so this chapter focuses on ways to reduce the impact of business. It contains simple suggestions for your immediate work environment as well as ideas for your boss. Many businesses understand their obligation to reduce their waste and create a liveable environment, and progressive business leaders know that they can save money and have more productive, engaged employees by instituting green policies. This chapter also has ideas for home entrepreneurs – in the UK, an additional 200,000 every year – who may shortchange themselves in health terms as they devote time and resources to developing their business.

Corporate Wellness

Up to 70 per cent of staff suffer health complaints related to their work environment. Some complaints are related to modern buildings – so-called 'sick building syndrome' – and others are caused by poorly arranged workstations and too much time at the computer. A friend tells me that in her office, 'Someone is always sick and we all get headaches. A couple of people are being treated for migraines.'

The best way to cope with a sedentary office job is to break up your day with exercise and regular stretching. Encourage your company to install bike racks and showers, subsidise gym memberships and provide healthier food and drinks. A positive trend in the workplace is 'corporate wellness' programmes. These include healthy cafeteria menus, exercise and sports facilities, and even stress management and meditation classes.

Computers

The number of workers using computers is growing all the time. Data entry clerks, secretaries, bank clerks, writers, stockbrokers and physicists spend their days in front of VDUs. Lower paid workers are more likely to spend unbroken time working directly on the screen and have less freedom to take rest breaks. Their output is sometimes directly monitored by the computer, which increases stress and makes it even more unlikely that they will take sufficient rest.

Some companies have policies that workers who use VDUs for more than 26 hours a week must have a 15-minute break every three hours. It also helps to have mobile keyboards, anti-glare screens and offices with diffuse overhead lighting. The VDU Workers' Rights Campaign suggests that no employee should spend more than four hours, or half the working day, at a VDU and that computers should be properly shielded. *(See Chapter 13 for practical suggestions.)*

TIPS: FOR ENCOURAGING HEALTHY FOOD AND EXERCISE

- Ask for, or offer, interest-free loans for public transport season tickets and transport expenses for cyclists.
- Encourage cycling to work by providing showers and bike racks.
- Try going out with colleagues for a brisk walk rather than a pint at lunch time.
- Stock the office kitchen with real glasses and mugs, and paper rather than plastic or polystyrene cups – you'll appreciate the difference.
- Ask for healthy drink alternatives: companies might be able to increase productivity by encouraging good snacking habits.
- Choose foods and bottled drinks packaged in glass rather than plastic.
- Choose washable cloth roller towels for kitchens and bathrooms.
- If you heat up food at lunch time, microwave only in glass or ceramic containers.
- Ask whoever orders the tea and coffee to switch to 'fair trade' products.

Products and Equipment

Some office products contain toxic solvents – stick to items which are odour-free and use water-based correction fluid and odourless water-based marker pens. It is also important to use non-toxic pens and glues – better for you and for the environment.

Purchase non-plastic equipment and office supplies when possible. Solid metal stationery trays, for example, cost more than the plastic equivalent, but they look good and last for ever. You should also make an effort to buy furniture made from temperate forest woods.

TIPS: **FOR IMPROVING YOUR PHYSICAL OFFICE SPACE**

- Design to reduce noise.
- Declare your office a no-smoking area.
- Switch from halon fire extinguishers to carbon dioxide ones.
- Install low-energy light bulbs, especially in wall and ceiling fixtures.
- Make the best use of natural lighting and natural ventilation for heating and cooling.
- Ensure there is good ventilation – and have windows that can be opened easily.
- Install ceiling fans – they use a fraction of the energy of air conditioners.
- Position desks by windows to increase daylighting. Full-spectrum bulbs can also help – spending seven hours a day under fluorescent lighting is not good for anyone.
- Use natural materials such as wood and rattan wherever possible.
- Allow new carpets to out-gas, with good ventilation, while rooms are unoccupied or install untreated carpets.
- Use latex rather than oil-based paint on walls and furniture.
- Check for sources of air pollution: art supplies, photocopiers, carpets, etc.
- Place photocopying machines and laser printers at a distance from work stations (they contain toners and solvents which you should avoid breathing).
- Have real plants in the office – they are good for the air and for the spirits. Increase the humidity by standing plants in trays of pebbles and water.

Recycling at Work

There are numerous ways in which we can reuse materials and cut down on the enormous waste created by the modern office. Try introducing some of the tips below into your office or suggest them to your boss, union and colleagues.

TIPS: FOR MINIMISING WASTE

Reduce
- Avoid over-packaged products – tell retailers that you prefer simple biodegradable packaging.
- Stop over-purchasing; encourage everyone to use things up and order only what they need.
- Send circulars rather than individual copies.

Reuse
- The cheapest, lightest packing material is *air*. Blow up a plastic bag or bin liner, rubberband it shut and use that. If you get styrofoam 'peanuts', complain and then reuse them or find someone else who can.
- Use string to tie packages rather than layers of plastic tape.
- Use green cleaning products and rechargeable batteries.
- Buy products than can be refilled or reconditioned (these include toner cartridges for laser printers and photocopying machines).
- Reuse envelopes whenever possible. My publishing business has its own adhesive post-consumer paper labels – contact us if you'd like a sample.
- Lease equipment, or try out someone else's.
- Buy used or remanufactured equipment and furniture.
- Use the second side of discarded office paper for rough drafts and notepads, and make double-sided printing a standard practice.
- Reuse files, ring binders, envelopes, etc., particularly for internal use and when presentation doesn't matter a great deal.
- Reuse packing materials and boxes, or find someone who needs them.

Recycle
- Use a plain paper fax machine rather than one that uses non-recyclable chemically-treated thermal paper.
- Have fax, inkjet and laser cartridges refilled, or return them for recycling, recharging or remanufacturing.
- Have your printing done with soya ink, on recycled paper. It's essential to buy recycled to create a market for recycled materials. *(Contact Hammets Recycled Stationery for personal stationery and a quote for your business; see Resources.)*
- Set up recycling bins for different types of paper, tins, glass, plastics and for things to donate to other businesses or local schools.
- Recycle your old computers. *(For information on what to do with office equipment you no longer need, go to http://www.creativelement.com/swap/.)*

Energy Impact

The best thing companies can do for the environment is to reduce drastically commuting by car and business travel by aeroplane. There are many ways to reduce commuting: providing incentives to use public transport and car-pooling, cutting car-related perks, encouraging employees to live near their workplace and supporting telecommuting by providing key employees with equipment for a home office. Major British companies are working with Transport 2000 on 'green commuter plans'. Shower facilities encourage workers to cycle.

TIPS: FOR SAVING ON ENERGY

- Co-ordinate packages sent by courier and, if you use mail order, order in bulk. Use electronic mail and fax, as well as ordinary mail, rather than courier services.
- Turn computers and other equipment off when not in use for a period of time, and use standby and energy-saving modes on electronic equipment.
- There is no point in heating unused areas; you can switch the heat to a lower setting, or off altogether, over weekends and holidays. Reduce the temperature in work areas by one or two degrees – people are less alert in overheated rooms. It also makes sense to install control units and radiator valves.
- Utilise daylight as much as possible and use energy-efficient, compact fluorescent bulbs.
- If you or your company have this amount of control over the building, insulate walls and draught-proof doors and windows.

Staying Personal

The latest thinking about business performance emphasises teamwork and communication, not simply individual effort and technological skills. People standing around the tea trolley may seem like an old-fashioned idea, but recent studies have found that when co-workers stop talking to one another informally – when they e-mail people who work on the same floor, even in the same room – business suffers. The health consequences of human isolation are well-documented. Progressive twenty-first-century businesses will make use of technology without forgetting that success depends upon real people living in real time. Dynamic global businesses make extensive use of information and communication technologies, but they also encourage people to exchange ideas and talk over problems face to face.

13

Technology
and
Communications

Nowadays we are surrounded by circuits and chips, in our watches and toasters, as well as TVs and computers. Like the genetic modification of foods, the development of new technologies is proceeding faster than most of us – even the professionals – can keep up with. Even in the United States, where scientific and technological advances are usually embraced without debate, people are now asking questions about what we will lose, as well as gain, from the latest technologies. Campaigns like the National TV Turn-Off Week are supported by the educational and medical establishments, and some farsighted techies have launched a campaign called Technorealism to think about how things like wristwatches that allow Internet connections and visual telephones will affect our lives and our society.

We cannot, individually, tame technology, but we can start to make choices about what makes sense for us in terms of health and environmental impact and human connections. I grew up in Silicon Valley in California and I'm now involved in electronic publishing, so I'm far from being a technophobe. But I do think we need to be careful about how we take on technologies. I use the term 'appropriate technology' to describe what we should aim for. This term used to apply to inexpensive technologies that could be used in developing countries – solar refrigerators and better ploughs, for example. While that meaning is still valid, I think it can also be applied to our use of computers and mobile phones.

This chapter is a survey of the technologies that affect us most – mobile phones, e-mail and the Internet. It also provides information about repetitive strain injury and ergonomics, our increasingly electric- and data-laden homes and airwaves, and related issues like light and noise pollution.

Technology and the Environment

The computer age was embraced by many environmentalists because they thought it would mean less resource use and less travel. Things haven't worked out that way. The more computers we have, the more paper we generate. The more businesses are connected by LANs (local area networks), WANs (wide area networks) and Intranet sites, the more business travel there is. Air miles have become a kind of global currency and the atmosphere above us is filled with planes at all times of day and night.

On the other hand, the global communications and the sharing of information through the Internet are a great boon to people working on environmental issues. They enable fast, cheap communication as well as sophisticated monitoring of current problems and the modelling of future environmental scenarios. Computers enable many people to work at home – running their own graphic design business, for example, or telecommuting. More and more professionals spend a day or two each week working from home. Companies get more productive employees, and telecommuters, their families and communities and the environment also benefit.

New technologies have also enabled people to move their businesses to rural areas, providing employment without adding traffic or noise. Considering the pressure on housing in the south-east of England, such relocation is important. But human factors weigh in: companies still want their employees in one place and people naturally congregate where there are many job opportunities.

In the sixties, people thought the computer business was wonderful because it was a clean industry. Today, the highest concentration of toxic waste sites, known as Superfund sites, in the United States is in Silicon Valley, the home of the computer industry. Producing computers uses natural resources, requires the use of many toxic chemicals, consumes an increasing amount of the world's energy and generates a great deal of waste.

Another important issue is our incessant quest for enough RAM and bigger hard drives. Every time computers get twice as fast, millions of people buy new machines and junk the old ones. *(For more about recycling computers, see page 143.)* Technology is also exclusionary: only a few will have the latest and the fastest, which contributes to the growing gulf between rich and poor nations.

Electric World

No one argues that nuclear (ionising) radiation is safe and measures are taken to protect us from it. But what of the non-ionising radiation – usually called 'electromagnetic frequencies (EMFs)' – that comes from equipment we use all the time?

We are exposed to EMFs from electrical equipment, power cables above our heads or running underground, microwaves and the TV and radio broadcasting networks which have become an essential part of our lives, and it isn't known whether these forms of energy are harmful to people. For one thing, military and industrial interests have prevented biologists from fully researching the effects of microwaves and radar, and the continued development of technology and wiring of the world depends on the assumption that there are no biological effects. Most of the time scientists attempt to reassure us, telling us not to worry until something is proven guilty by lengthy tests or when the evidence in the environment is irrefutable.

In the future, we're likely to see houses designed to minimise EMFs, but in the meantime we have to do what we can ourselves. Think about ways to reduce your 'electric load'.

TIPS: FOR REDUCING EXPOSURE TO EMFS

- Keep all equipment at a distance.
- Choose non-electrical equipment whenever possible and multi-use equipment (a combined fax/answering machine, for example).
- Minimise the electrical equipment in your bedroom. Keep all electrical equipment and cords at least four feet from your bed. A ceiling or wall-mounted light is best.
- Turn off and unplug equipment not in use (TVs, videos).
- If you have to keep your mobile phone with you, put it as far as possible from your gonads and head.
- Look for non-ionising smoke detectors.

Ionisers

Air-conditioning and heating systems, cigarette smoke, synthetic carpeting and electronic equipment of all kinds change the balance of ions in the air. A positive charge is associated with increased susceptibility to illness, including hay fever and migraine headaches. Seaside air is invigorating because of its negative ion charge.

Using fewer electrical appliances and more natural materials in your home, along with good ventilation, may solve part of the problem, but an ioniser, which creates a negative charge in the air, makes a perceptible improvement in the indoor environment for many people. Ionisers are relatively inexpensive and use very little power. Alternatively, indoor plants are a completely low-tech way to improve air quality.

Communications

In a few years, a global system of electronic connections has altered the way we communicate with friends and family, how we meet people with common interests, how we answer our own and our children's questions and how we do our jobs.

>The Internet

The Internet, and its locator system the World Wide Web, is an unprecedented source of information and contacts, pornography and craziness. It's both a great time saver – when you want to look up some government statistic – and the biggest time waster ever invented. It's also a system that hasn't even reached adolescence. It's likely to improve in many ways (the most important of which will be systems to filter out all the rubbish) and to decline in others, especially as users are encouraged to exchange their time, sitting and watching adverts, for free e-mail or free computers.

Women have been slower than men to move to the Web, perhaps because they are less confident about dealing with the machinery and software involved, or maybe because they are more likely to instinctively value personal, local connections. But from a mere 10 per cent of online users only a few years ago, women's online presence has quadrupled in some countries. Many observers think that this will change the nature of Internet interactions, as women demand both different content and more user-friendly systems. Women are also becoming involved in technology because they have to provide kids with computers and help with homework. (Many health experts and educators are concerned about the effects of computers on young children; see pages 195–6.)

>E-mail

E-mail is the new technology that appeals to most people. It's quick, cheap and convenient and brings old friends and far-flung families into regular contact. It has some drawbacks, though. For one thing, it costs companies a lot in lost employee time, as people spend working hours e-mailing friends and sending jokes. It allows computer viruses to spread rapidly and it doesn't promote the thoughtful exchange that old-fashioned letters did. I've never seen anyone get the same pleasure from an e-mail that we used to get out of a long letter from a distant friend and a handwritten love letter has a lot more impact that an e-mail printout. People still buy writing paper and the fountain pen business is booming, so maybe we will manage to preserve and develop both forms of communication.

>E-commerce

We don't know how e-commerce is going to change our lives or whether it's ever going to make money for the investors throwing billions into it. Many of us don't know whether it's safe to use a credit card over the Internet and what impact e-commerce will have on the environment.

There are two great dangers in e-commerce. First, it may encourage people to become even more obsessed with shopping, as they find more things to want. Eco living, on the other hand, is about getting focused, thinking about what you really need and what will truly add to your quality of life, keeping possessions to a reasonable, sustainable level.

Secondly, e-commerce does away with the personal connections involved in shopping. For some people, that's the appeal of online shopping. But vibrant towns and neighbourhoods depend on active local commerce, and to reduce the impact of transport on the environment we need, as far as possible, to buy food and goods that are grown or made and sold locally.

The electronic auction, in which individuals bid on items for sale – ranging from an antique doll to a brand new software program – on an auction website, has potential, as does online bartering, with companies as well as individuals participating.

Environmentalists have always promoted second-hand shopping and barter as good ways to reduce our overall consumption. But it's been difficult to link the person who no longer needs a particular item with the person who'd love to buy it. Online services may be the answer. Even better, online community bulletin boards could facilitate local selling and bartering.

Mobile Communications

In addition to mobile phones we may soon be using computers that connect to the Internet via cellular towers, so our personal exposure to low-level electronic magnetic frequencies is going to grow. Some scientists say that low-level EMFs cannot be dangerous, simply because they are low level. Others look at odd findings – people whose reaction times speeded up and rats which binged on alcohol after being exposed to microwaves – and want to know what the long-term health effects are going to be. A 1999 survey of studies related to mobile phones found that researchers don't know how to interpret some of the results they're getting and that it's been extremely difficult to reproduce studies in different labs. Since the replication of results is the basis of scientific agreement, the area is fraught with uncertainty.

What do we know? In tests, cells and worms react to mobile frequencies by multiplying or growing faster. This suggests a possible link with cancer, but none of the standard carcinogen tests have so far shown that the EMFs from mobiles cause cancer. In any case, carcinogens don't cause cancer overnight. What makes them difficult to track, and prove, is that exposure may result in cancer ten or twenty years later, even if the source of the carcinogen has been removed. And it is almost impossible to prove a direct correlation between a source and a disease – unless you have a huge pool of people, like smokers, to draw from.

What is clear so far is that our bodies are not used to being bombarded with EMFs and that a variety of symptoms, from fatigue to short-term memory loss, could be associated with this exposure. Some 500 million people now use mobile phones and the number is growing rapidly. Unlike most equipment, they stay very close to our bodies, sometimes twenty-four hours a day, and in the long run they may provide more information on the effects of EMFs on human beings than anything else. But you don't want to be a guinea pig. Scientists say that until we know more it makes sense to keep your exposure as low as possible.

Cellular Towers and Broad Band

Communications networks are changing our world not just socially or professionally, but environmentally. This area is so new, and so subtle, that it's received little attention. But in the twenty-first century we're likely to hear about a new form of air pollution: the waves and signals that send vast amounts of data flowing around the world.

The buzzword is 'broad-band' content, that is, services – television, movies, music, information – that are data-intensive. Broad-band multimedia applications require ways of moving huge amounts of digital information. The telephone lines that enable most of the new communications technologies we are familiar with – from faxes to Internet connections to mobile phones – aren't enough, so companies are aiming at Internet access that is both wired and wire-less to provide content for money to users all over the world. These methods include radio and microwave transmission, various forms of satellite service, interactive cable, fixed wireless, broad-band cellular and cable television lines and fast ISDN phone lines.

Not only do these technologies mean damage to trees and hedges and death to thousands of birds attracted to the lights of communications towers, but they will also dramatically increase the level of the EMF, radio and microwave frequencies to which we are exposed. No one knows how this will affect us, or plants and animals and natural cycles.

Computers

Some specialists insist that computers are completely safe and that the symptoms reported by modern office workers around the world – headaches, dry eyes, excessive fatigue – are the result of personal or other environmental factors. Other researchers conclude that health risks like eye irritation, headaches and muscle aches (commonly called repetitive strain injury) are directly related to the constant use of computer terminals, combined with poor lighting, posture and the physical set up of the workspace.

Computers are so common that an acceptance that they can cause health problems presents considerable practical issues for government and companies. The reality is that most of us who work with computers know that they affect us, and eye specialists and other doctors who deal with people all the time also accept that there are common syndromes associated with computer use. While more studies are being done, there is much we can do to make our working lives more comfortable.

>Machine Fatigue

Years ago, typists sometimes got sore necks, but they didn't get repetitive strain injury (RSI), the debilitating problem that results from performing the same tiny movement for hours on end. RSI, also known as carpal tunnel syndrome for the carpal nerve that is compressed, afflicts the growing millions of people who spend their workdays using a keyboard or mouse, as well as chicken pluckers and seamstresses who work by hand.

The warning signs are a tingling in your wrists and hand pain. Unfortunately, RSI often strikes with little warning after a long bout of intense keyboard work so it's very important to take preventative measures before you feel any symptoms. Forward-thinking employers are willing to help workers arrange their workplaces to prevent injury. There is a direct connection between your physical health at work and your performance, so it is important that employers and employees take steps to improve work space (*see Chapter 12 for suggestions*).

The problem most often reported among computer users is eye strain. Upper body tension and lower back pain are also common. It's essential to adjust your computer screen, as well as your keyboard, to your body. Many companies are designing keyboards, mice and mousepads that create less strain on users and the new flat screens should be easier on us than current cathode ray units. But it's going to be a long time before we all have access to them. In the meantime, we need to look for ways to decrease machine fatigue through thoughtful arrangements and good work habits.

TIPS: FOR WORKING ON A COMPUTER

- Position yourself 18–24 inches from the screen with your eyes 6–8 inches above the centre of the screen.
- Your knees should be level with your thighs – try putting a book underneath your feet.
- Your chair should support the natural curve of your back. Don't slouch.
- Eliminate glare through changing the screen position or with an anti-glare screen.
- Eliminate static with an anti-static mat, water spray or bowl of water and plants.
- Clean your screen, your glasses and contact lenses frequently.
- If overhead fluorescent lights bother you, try a desk lamp with a 100w bulb.
- Blink every three to five seconds – computer users tend to forget to blink and their eyes get dry – and use eye drops if necessary.

- Look away from your computer screen frequently, at least every five minutes.
- Move your eyes. Look out the window or even at a picture on a distant wall. You might want to put a mirror near your screen to create additional visual distance.
- Your fingers should be level with or below your wrists and your wrists level with or below your elbows
- Take a break at least every half an hour. Get up and move around.
- Exercise: stretch your arms overhead, lean forward to touch your toes and stretch out your back and hamstrings *(see also below)*.
- Vary your work: switch from task to task at regular intervals.
- Use the keyboard commands instead of the mouse.
- Stand up. I've solved my computer-related back pain by putting my computer on a raised desk, so I stand and type. Standing also encourages me to move around more frequently.
- Find an old manual typewriter and use it for personal letters or a diary. Typing on a manual machine is fantastic exercise for the hands – and it's fun.
- Regular yoga practice has been found to relieve RSI symptoms. There are many stretching and strengthening yoga positions that work the hands and wrists, so ask your teacher about them.
- Postures that put downward pressure on your hands are especially good. Maybe you can do a handstand behind your office door, or just press your hands flat into the wall to stretch out fingers and wrists.

>Exercises

There are many exercises that can be done at your desk to help relieve eye strain and other computer-related injuries:

(1) Close your eyes, relax your face and brow, and move your eyes from side to side while breathing deeply.
(2) Exercise your eyes by shifting them in corner-to-corner patterns on your screen.
(3) To release tension and wake up the eyes, inhale deeply and squeeze your eyes shut as tightly as you can while tightening

your jaw, face and neck. Exhale quickly while stretching your eyes and mouth wide open.

(4) To release tension in your fingers and hands, drop them to your sides and shake them for about 15 seconds. Then extend your fingers as far as you can a few times and rotate your wrists front to back.

(5) For general aches and pains throughout the day, roll your head in full circles whenever you have a chance. Stand up and stretch both hands above the head, pressing your feet hard into the floor.

(6) Massage your temples and the base of your head above the neck for relief of neck strain.

(7) Close your eyes and rub your earlobes, or squeeze the bridge between your eyes, to relieve a headache.

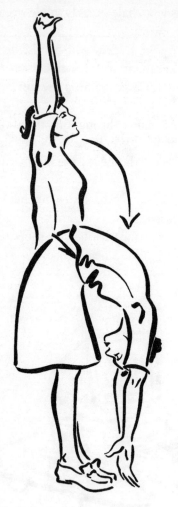

Stretch your arms
overhead. Lean forward to
touch your toes and stretch
your back and hamstrings.

Noise

Wherever you live, the volume of sound in your environment will
have increased substantially over the past seventy years or so.
Sound, for our ancestors, provided useful information about the
environment. The crack of thunder or the sound of falling rocks

were signals which helped them to deal with the world around them. Most of the noise (unwanted or undesirable sound) we face today tells us nothing meaningful, but our bodies still instinctively treat loud sounds as warning signals. Our hearts beat faster, our breathing speeds up and muscles tense. These reactions can lead to a wide range of health problems, from high blood pressure and headaches to ulcers, cardiovascular disease and disturbed sleep.

Q Studies have shown that people living near an airport visit the doctor two to three times more often than average and suffer increased rates of high blood pressure, heart disease and psychological problems.

TIPS: FOR QUIETENING YOUR LIFE

- Unplug unused equipment to stop low-level humming.
- Use your energy instead of a power station's – try using a broom or carpet sweeper, a hand-operated pencil sharpener or coffee grinder.
- Choose quiet appliances and place rubber mats underneath noisy fridges, typewriters and other sources of domestic noise.
- Negotiate a music agreement – times of day and maximum levels on the volume control.
- Plant hedges or rows of trees to muffle traffic noise.
- Use building features such as sealed double-pane glass, shutters and solid doors, walls and floors to block out noise. Cupboards built between rooms provide excellent soundproofing.
- Place heavy furniture, like old-fashioned wooden wardrobes, against shared walls.
- Energy-saving insulation cuts down on noise as well as heat loss, as do soft furnishings, carpets and wall hangings.
- Wear earplugs in noisy environments rather than just tolerate an uncomfortable situation.
- Spend some time in places where it is really quiet. It's a challenge to get completely beyond the sound of cars (you might have to do some walking to get there), but well worth it.

Let noise be a consideration when you choose where to live. Visit a prospective home at different times of day and at weekends.

Light Pollution

Going out on a summer's night to watch an eclipse or a meteor shower is one of the best ways to connect with the beauty and mystery of the universe. If you live near a city, though, you've lost the view that everyone on Earth used to share, not only because of air pollution but because of something only astronomers talk about a lot: light pollution.

In the 1950s the Royal Observatory at Greenwich had to move to Sussex because of light pollution. In the 1980s it was moved to the Canary Islands, where the Spanish authorities have passed laws and modified street lights to protect the night sky. A public campaign used the slogan: 'Put out a light, switch on a star.'

The International Dark Sky Association is working on ways to stop the environmental impact of light pollution (which goes hand-in-hand with energy saving) and limit space debris. This is an area in which governments and businesses have to take action, but individuals can help by using automatic timers to put lights on only when needed, directing lights downwards and installing energy-efficient, low-pressure sodium (LPS) lights.

Q While the scare over nightlights causing near-sightedness was unfounded, there does seem to be a biological need for darkness when we sleep.

Taming Technology

We've all heard arguments about the pub-like atmosphere of Internet chat rooms and special interest e-mail lists, and I know some people find a sense of camaraderie on the Web. But I also see friends who distance themselves from the rough and tumble of actual relationships by relying on the comfort of the manageable friendships of the Web. What about when you need someone right now? Imagine a world where you've just found out your mother is dying or your partner has dumped you and the only way to get hold of your friends is via e-mail or the voice mail on their mobile.

I am a technological moderate: I use computers all the time, enjoy regular e-mail communications with people all over the world and find the Web a marvellous source of information. But when it comes to relationships, what matters is being able to share a meal or go on a long walk together. I've certainly got long-term and friendly professional relationships started by e-mail, but I don't look for friends on the Web.

Over time, we will be able to see more clearly the limits of new technologies and we need to be confident enough to reject the things that don't work – for us, for society or for the environment.

TIPS: FOR ENRICHING YOUR PERSONAL LIFE

- Preserve memories on paper (acid-free if possible). Computer disks and videotapes have a lifespan of only five to seven years; paper will last for centuries.
- Go to live concerts, lectures and sports matches.
- Make a serious effort to find people close at hand who share your interests.
- Get involved in local politics.
- Ask a friend for help.
- Offer to help a neighbour out.
- Remind yourself that in-the-flesh relationships, messy as they are, are essential to psychological health. Enjoy them.

14

Travel and Holidays

E co living doesn't always mean simple choices. While the greenest holiday is taken close to home, because travelling to other parts of the country or world uses lots of energy and resources, there is a lot we can learn through travel.

Tourism is the world's largest industry, with annual revenues of over US $400 billion. It employs one in fifteen of the world's workers. But aeroplanes contribute tonnes of carbon dioxide to the atmosphere each year and a considerable percentage of total climate-altering gases. In addition, 60 per cent of ozone-destroying gases come from aircraft – and things are getting worse.

The travel and tourism sectors are amongst the fastest growing areas of the economy in many countries, both rich and poor. It is essential that we find ways to minimise the damage they do and maximise the social and economic benefits they can bring.

Q The number of tourists is expected to triple in the next ten years, to an annual one billion people. Revenues will quadruple, but what of the pollution?

Eco Tourism

Many of us go on holiday looking for pure escape – quiet, peace and starlit skies at night. But if millions of us travel the globe looking for remote retreats, *nowhere* will be remote and it'll be impossible ever to find a retreat.

We take our world with us and too often destroy the thing we love. In fact, a recent WWF study found that some of the most profitable tourist destinations – Spain, Florida and the Alps – are going to be dramatically affected and perhaps ruined by global warming. Malarial mosquitoes are surging north, coastal areas may flood and there will be less snow. Increasingly violent storms, hurricanes and earthquakes will play havoc with airlines and holiday schedules.

All over the world, visitors and investors are destroying the real life of regions. Local customs and religious rituals are transformed into spectacles, and traditional crafts become souvenirs. The ecosystem balance is disrupted by beach developments, mountain chalets and ski areas, and even wilderness areas that have to be reached on foot are being littered and eroded. Family and community ties are broken as people become dependent on outsiders for their livelihood.

Tourism does not bring prosperity to poor regions. The tourist industry generates only unskilled jobs – responsible positions tend to go to foreign employees – and 80 per cent of the money spent on holidays comes back to the home countries, in foreign staff salaries, foreign-owned hotel profits, travel agency commissions, payment for imported food and other items, insurance and interest on loans. Most of the remaining 20 per cent goes to a few wealthy locals and government officials.

But travel is, or can be, broadening. It helps us to understand our global village and appreciate the material wealth we enjoy. Many people travel to learn – about history, other cultures or the natural world. There are beautiful things – human-made and natural – to be enjoyed and appreciated everywhere.

The solution is to travel less frequently and more slowly. Rushing off to Costa Rica for a week is not ecological tourism. Also, remember that every pound you take – on a plane or in a car – takes extra fuel to move. Don't try to get around weight restrictions. And when you're packing to come home, remember that rule for wilderness travel: 'Take nothing but photographs and leave nothing but footprints.' Don't go crazy with photographs, either – conventional film processing is a polluting business (though eco-labs recycle canisters and film cassettes, recover silver and put no chemicals down the drain). Choose one or two wonderful souvenirs and if you're in the developing world, consider travelling with some decent clothes you can leave behind with a charitable institution.

Health in the Air

Airlines face intense competition to keep profits high and today's flights are packed full, with seats set ever closer together. You've probably read reports about the increase in 'air rage'. Is this because more hooligans are flying or are we losing the ability to cope with other people at close quarters?

While this may be partially true, another explanation is that people are suffering the effects of oxygen deprivation as airlines cut costs by using ventilation systems that draw in less than 50 per cent fresh air, recycling the rest throughout a flight. Recycling air makes a plane more energy-efficient, but puts passenger health in jeopardy. The Aviation Health Institute claims that cabin air quality has declined so precipitously that passengers suffer, in effect, from carbon dioxide poisoning. This can cause physical discomfort as well as anxiety attacks, mood swings and palpitations.

On a non-smoking flight, it is impossible to tell how stale the air is. We need to encourage governments to monitor air quality standards on aircraft in the hope that it won't become necessary for all of us to travel with oxygen inhalers.

TIPS: FOR FLYING

- Avoid dehydration: drink lots of water, avoid alcohol and bring along a spray bottle of water to keep your skin moist.
- Breathe deeply to maximise your oxygen intake.
- Take shorter flights and if you have a chance to get off the plane do so – walk or jog around the airport, or get outside for some fresh air if you can.
- Ring ahead and order vegetarian meals.
- You see more wasteful packaging and disposable products on aeroplanes than anywhere else – turn down all the over-packaged extras and write to the airline asking for better environmental policies.
- When you arrive, spend as much time as possible in daylight. This will enable your internal clock to reset itself and you'll recover from jetlag more quickly.

Food on the Go

Most of the food available when you're on the road is heavily processed, over-packaged and unhealthy. You can enjoy better food and save money by ensuring that you always have basic picnic equipment in your glove compartment or overnight case (a sharp knife; corkscrew; a few pieces of cutlery; small hand towels to use as napkins and for wiping up; salt and pepper). During the day, you can stop at a market or shop to buy provisions.

If you're driving, take along real mugs and wine glasses to avoid getting takeaway coffee or tea in a plastic cup (saves waste and tastes much better). Best of all, equip an old-fashioned wicker picnic basket with a tiny camp stove. For long journeys, I love to take a big flask of hot apple juice spiked with cinnamon. Firm bread, biscuits, cheese, fresh fruit, raw vegetables and dried fruit and nuts travel well and enough can be tucked into a handbag or briefcase for a light lunch or supper.

Eat local specialities and look for locally owned small restaurants off the main tourist strip. (There are Slow Food guides to restaurants for some countries.)

Even on holiday you can sometimes separate waste. Ask where to recycle newspapers. Toss apple cores into the woods and empty your coffee flask over plants.

Hotels

Hotels are massive consumers of water, energy and materials. But some hotel chains realise that they can improve public relations and save money by initiating 'green hotel' policies. These include installing energy-efficient light bulbs and heating systems, water-saving toilet devices and body-care product dispensers instead of all those miniature bottles. They display cards offering you the choice not to have your bed and towels changed daily, and remind guests to turn off the air conditioner when they leave the room.

Working Holidays

One of the mantras of educationalists and even politicians these days is 'life-long learning'. The idea is that in this age of rapid technological and social change, no degree can prepare you for the world, and job market, of the future. All of us need to keep on learning and one way is by taking working or 'service' holidays. This is a switch from the kind of holiday where you just throw yourself on the sand to relax for two weeks, but the old saying 'a change is as good as a rest' may be true for you. These holidays are not luxury breaks by any means, but they can provide a real change from routine and a sense of how other people live.

If you've always wondered what it would be like to live on a farm and grow your own food, for example, you could go to an organic farm and help with planting or harvesting. And if you feel caught up in a materialistic world, the perfect escape might be helping in a soup kitchen or working with disadvantaged kids in another part of the country.

Holiday time can also be used to explore new options. As our lives become increasingly comfortable and affluent, more of us are thinking about the question of meaning. Is it possible to make a living and find a sense of purpose at the same time? Recent surveys show that more college graduates are thinking about their careers in terms of satisfaction and meaning – making a difference. You might want to go into politics and work for more sustainable economic policies, or into environmental law, or ethical investment, and be able to use a holiday to gain some experience of your chosen field or awareness of other career alternatives.

Become an Amateur Anthropologist

My husband David is an anthropologist and I asked him for some tips for travellers on how to learn about – and from – the local people, whether you're visiting Bali or Florida. 'The most important thing to remember,' he said, 'is that almost everyone is thrilled to have someone take a sincere interest in their way of life.'

Sincerity and genuine interest are quickly recognised around the world and received with hospitality and openness. David has had students who have watched the sacred January deer dance with Taos Indian women from pueblo rooftops in Taos, New Mexico, eat in pueblo homes, and dance and eat with Puerto Rican men and women in local restaurants off the tourist track in the central mountains. None of these events were planned, but all of the participants felt that their experience was more truly memorable because of the opportunity to interact with the local people.

The key to having a true local experience is to approach it in manner that fits with your lifestyle. Some people prefer to stay in familiar tourist hotels, eat in tourist restaurants and visit only the major attractions. Others go to the other extreme and want to 'go native' and live as much as possible as if they are a local. For most people, a more middle-ground approach that combines genuine involvement in local culture with at least some Western amenities allows for the richest experience. The truth is that you cannot observe or participate much if you are worried abut the water and food, or feel uncomfortable because you don't understand the language, so wander off the tourist track only as far as you can reasonably manage.

Prepare for a trip by reading about and, if you possibly can, by talking to someone familiar with the place you are going to. Standard guidebooks aren't much help when it comes to culture and you may get more from current non-fiction books or even novels set in the place you're visiting. Check the Web, too, for information that goes beyond the usual lists of hotels.

TIPS: FOR THOUGHTFUL TRAVEL

- Find out about where you are going. Buy or borrow a good guide book or a novel set in the area.
- Try train rather than car or plane. Could you travel some of the way on foot or by bicycle?
- Instead of 'doing' sights or countries, choose a spot which has a genuine interest for you or your family.
- Try to find a connection with a local person – through a colleague, old friend or the Internet. Many people are thrilled to be able to show their home to a visitor and even if you just meet for dinner and a walk, your experience will be far richer.
- Make a home exchange (www.homeexchange.com and many others) – you'll save money and through your exchange partners meet neighbours, get recommendations about local specialities and have a richer experience.

- Avoid the mobile ghetto of package tours, which give tourists no contact with anyone whose job is not taking care of them. If you do want to use a tour company, go to one that is alert to ecological and ethical issues in tourism *(contact Tourism Concern for advice; see Resources)*.
- Instead of looking for home-from-home in a Western-style hotel, experience something different from your regular way of life.
- Stay in B & Bs and small owner-run hotels instead of chain hotels, to put your money into the local economy.
- Choose hotels with 'green' policies and fill out comment cards to encourage them.
- Don't over-use towels and hot water just because you're not paying extra for them.
- Leave those little bottles of shampoo at the hotel; they are wasteful packaging and you don't need them.
- Turn off lights and turn down heating and air conditioning.

Keeping A Pet

(15)

What role should animals play in our lives? The petkeeping that we in Europe and North America indulge in is not particularly sound in terms of our impact on the natural world. Keeping cats and dogs adds to pollution and the overall consumption demands on the planet. Think of all those plastic packets of dog food and rubber toys and cat litter, the noise and mess caused by dogs in cities, the wildlife killed by domestic cats.

Yet having animals around reflects a genuine ecological need – for connection with other species and thus with the natural world. Most children are thrilled by almost any kind of animal and there is evidence that animals may play an important role in children's emotional development. It's likely that humans instinctively seek out contact with other species, yet modern life essentially isolates us. Even in the countryside the sight of a pig rolling in the dirt or a flock of chicken scratching for insects has become a rarity thanks to factory farming.

Pets offer companionship to people who live on their own or who do not have a supportive family or community network. A dog offers protection without turning your home into a fortress, though an unhappy, barking dog is both a nuisance to neighbours and a potential danger. Britain is fortunate in not having to worry about rabies in the estimated 400,000 dog bites that occur each year, but there are numerous news reports of children mauled and permanently disfigured by previously docile animals.

None the less, keeping a pet clearly provides something we value. More than half the households in Britain have at least one cat or dog, and the more children in a family, the more pets they are likely to have. The emphasis of this chapter is on how to reduce, rather than eliminate, the environmental impact of your cat or dog or other pets.

Q In spite of the British reputation as animal lovers, some 350,000 dogs are put down every year (that is nearly 1,000 every day), and the RSPCA estimates that there are 500,000 unwanted dogs roaming our streets.

Pets and the Environment

The fact is that our pets consume vast amounts of food while people go hungry. More than £50 million is spent each year advertising pet foods and the range of products designed to tempt our fussy companions is growing. (This is a phenomenon seen only in North America and Western Europe; throughout the rest of the world, cats and dogs live on scraps and leftovers, or are expected to fend for themselves.)

Reducing the meat *we* consume is one of the most important steps in reducing air pollution and limiting global warming, so it's unfortunate that the pets we like most are carnivorous. Other animals are raised and slaughtered to feed our pets. It takes approximately 10lb of vegetable or grain protein to produce 1lb of animal protein and the grain used to feed livestock is often imported from Third World countries. In addition, 80 per cent of owners buy tinned pet food – an estimated two billion cans every year. The packaging and the energy used in processing and shipping petfood and products are more environmental costs.

Feeding Dogs and Cats

Many familiar commercial pet foods are the equivalent of junk food meals – appealing and addictive, but a nutritional and environmental disaster, full of fat, sugar, salt and fillers. Wholefood shops and veterinarians sell higher-quality additive-free products. The best-quality dried foods are a complete diet and are sympathetically packaged in cardboard or paper. Dry foods are also lighter, which means lower transport costs (and energy consumption).

Some people believe that cats and dogs should have a truly natural diet – fresh and raw, not cooked or dried and preserved with chemicals. One pet writer reported that animals on a natural diet (offal and meat) eat approximately one third less and, incidentally, produce far fewer faeces.

If you start from birth, it is possible to raise a dog as a vegetarian; the Vegetarian Society will provide detailed information sheets. A vegetarian diet would not work for cats, however, because it would be deficient in arachidonic acid, an essential fatty acid found in the structural fats of meat and fish. The Vegetarian Society urges vegetarian cat owners 'to consider whether their beliefs are consistent with risking jeopardising the health of any animal, or whether they should ask any animal to adapt its natural diet to suit the philosophy of the owner, no matter how noble the cause'.

Pet Pests

Pet fleas can be controlled without the dangerous insecticides in commercial flea sprays, powders and collars. I appreciate the ease of the new high-tech pill treatments that stop fleas from reproducing, but you may want to use a completely natural herbal and cleaning process.

If your pet has fleas, the first step in treatment is to vacuum thoroughly: carpets, rugs, upholstery, cushions and mattresses. Seal the vacuum bag in an old plastic bag and throw it away or burn it. Put your bedding, pet's bedding and rugs through a hot wash. Go through this routine again after three or four days.

Next, add nutritional yeast to your pet's food. This will make the pet taste nasty to fleas and improve its coat. Adding a few drops of cider vinegar to pets' drinking water is said to be helpful too, as is a daily dose of fresh garlic. Some breeders report using nothing but garlic to prevent roundworm.

The most sophisticated US research into non-toxic flea control has centred on components of citrus peels, which are said to kill all stages of the flea, from egg to adult.

A mint called pennyroyal is also a fleabane. Pennyroyal is a pretty plant with tiny leaves. Plant it all around the garden – plants can be divided as they spread – and use the dried leaves to pack a fabric flea collar. You can also buy pennyroyal oil to dab on a collar or bedding (this has caused rare cases of miscarriage, so don't try this if you have a pregnant pet or are pregnant yourself). You can also give your pet a rinse with strong (cool) pennyroyal tea after a bath.

Q About one million gallons of dog urine and 100 tons of faeces are left on our streets every day.

Ground Rules for Dogs

While dogs provide companionship, their faeces can be dangerous. According to the Hospital for Tropical Diseases, up to 100 children in Britain suffer eye damage every year as a result of *Toxocara canis*, a roundworm which is transmitted in dog faeces.

Toxocara can be carried on shoes and pram wheels and survives for several days on the floor.

If you move house, find out whether dogs – or cats, which also carry *Toxocara* – have had access to the garden. *Toxocara* can survive in soil for over two years. In one tragic case, a little girl went blind after her family moved into a house which had been an RSPCA shelter. Councils are moving towards more stringent controls and many parks now have dog-free areas and litter bins especially for faeces.

TIPS: FOR DOG CARE

- Get advice from your vet on worming to eliminate *Toxocara*.
- Carry a pooper-scooper or eco-friendly paper bag (check with your pet shop), or newspaper or an old carrier bag to clean up after your dog.
- Waste should be put into the rubbish bin or, preferably, flushed down the toilet.
- If you get a puppy, train it to defecate in a box or tray.
- If you live in the city where there are a great many dog faeces on the pavements, remove all shoes at the door and do not wheel prams into the house.

Cat Care

Cats are very popular pets but they can have a devastating impact on local wildlife. A recent report found that small mammals are their major prey. Birds came in second place, presumably because they are more difficult to catch, but a third to half of all sparrow deaths in the areas surveyed had been caused by house cats.

Wild animals, from hedgehogs to slow worms, are having a tough time as it is. We aren't killing birds with DDT any longer, but we are destroying their habitats. Our cats may be the final straw for some species. Put a bell on your cat so its prey can hear it coming and escape in time.

Using ecological cat litter is also a good idea. Our cats are happy with one made of wheat hulls (rough bran!) This can actually be composted, to use on flower (not vegetable) beds.

Pregnant women should avoid cat litter and gardens where cats defecate because of the risk of contacting *Toxoplasma*, a 'flu-like disease that can be passed to a foetus, causing serious mental or physical problems.

Smaller Pets

Choosing a small pet has many practical and environmental advantages. Hamsters and guinea pigs are bred in captivity, they can live on scraps from the kitchen and their overall environmental impact is slight in comparison with that of cats and dogs. If you keep rodents, though, it's important to ensure that they do not escape into the wild, where they can disturb the balance of the local ecosystem.

Britain is one of the nations that signed the Convention on International Trade in Endangered Species of Wild Fauna and Flora (CITES) in 1976. In spite of this, many animals popular in the pet trade, from lizards, pythons and iguanas to parrots and marine fish, are becoming rare or endangered. If you choose to keep a bird or reptile as a pet, ensure that it was bred in captivity.

If you have an aquarium, choose freshwater fish. Marine fish are always wild-caught (they are caught with cyanide-based drugs, as well as with nets) and a huge proportion die during shipment. Their life expectancy in an aquarium is only a few months. Goldfish, koi and freshwater tropical fish like guppies are an acceptable choice because they are bred in captivity. As one wildlife officer commented, 'We do not believe wild animals should be used as consumer durables.'

TIPS: FOR PET CARE

- Try not to depend on pets for security and companionship.
- Think small: big dogs are comparable to big cars in terms of expense and environmental impact. Small dogs also cope better with urban environments.
- Stick to one or two animals.
- Don't allow them to procreate.
- Prevent your pets from harassing or killing birds or other wildlife.
- Don't allow them to be fussy about food.
- Consider a vegetarian diet for dogs (this is not safe for cats).
- Use dried food because it has less packaging and weighs less.
- Keep equipment to a minimum.

Q City farms, which can be found all over Britain, provide employment and give children and older people a chance to experience something of the life of a farm and to eat locally raised food.

16

Having A Baby

I f you have children, you know how many choices you make on their behalf, with their future in mind. But few parents consider the ways in which environmental problems in the news today will have to be faced and dealt with by our children and grandchildren. We are only beginning to see the consequences of air pollution and global warming, nuclear contamination of the seas and the breakdown of the ozone layer. Parenthood can jog us into a new awareness of the world and a concern about the environment we live in.

The way we give birth is itself an ecological issue because proponents of modern birth technologies tend to see the ability to bear children, one of the primary cycles of the natural world, as insufficient and inefficient. The explosion of interest in natural childbirth in recent years is a sign, however, that many women are unwilling to see birth as a medical procedure. We need to learn from nature, instead of thinking that humans always know best. We also need to learn to limit our interference in a natural process – whether it is having a baby or the spring flooding of wetlands.

The Choice to Have Children

Children are a precious responsibility and a source of delight and challenge. We should think carefully about having them and raise them with a sense of responsibility towards others and towards the natural world.

Population has always been an important issue for environmentalists. Restricting human numbers is a vital part of improving the prospects for humankind. Amongst environmentalists and poverty groups there tends to be a division between those who advocate improved access to contraception as the primary tool for reducing population and those who emphasise poverty reduction, improvements in the status of women or economic development. This polarisation may obscure the fact that women around the world want to be able to choose not only whether but when to have children.

No option is perfect. The Pill and other hormonal methods are associated with a range of health problems. IUDs have been the subject of dozens of court cases and massive settlements in the US. Other methods, such as the diaphragm, require the use of chemical spermicides, with their attendant health risks. Abortion is an essential part of an effective reproductive health-care system, but it should be the option of last resort. Voluntary sterilisation is effective and relatively cheap, but it is not reversible and in many cases in the developing world it has not been voluntary. *(See also Green Sex, page 60.)*

Preparing for Birth

Before any pregnancy, both partners should make every effort to improve their diet, get fit and reduce their exposure to pollution of all kinds, thereby ensuring the healthiest possible conception. In some countries, there are regulations protecting people of childbearing age from hazardous chemical exposure at work. Once a woman is pregnant, of course she should eat a healthy diet and avoid tobacco, alcohol and drugs. Pregnant women should also avoid hazardous household chemicals, including pesticides, fertilisers, cleaning products and contact adhesive. Be especially careful at your workplace and while you're breastfeeding. *(Contact the London Hazards Centre or Foresight for more details; see Resources.)*

Q Environmental hazards thought to be damaging to the foetal brain include lead, heavy metals such as cadmium and mercury, solvents and PCBs.

TIPS: FOR PREGNANCY

- Avoid all medication (many common drugs have been shown to have a deleterious effect on the developing foetus).
- Stay away from food additives, including artificial sweeteners.
- Eat organic foods, especially meat (lean cuts, as pesticides, hormones and antibiotics concentrate in fatty tissue).
- Limit tea and coffee intake.
- Avoid alcohol.
- Do not paint the nursery at the last moment: it should smell of nothing but fresh air and sunshine.

Q For several years, US obstetricians have been warning pregnant women against using any chemical hair treatment.

>Ultrasound

Prospective parents have become used to regular ultrasound pictures of their developing baby, but the routine use of this technology troubles some observers. Critics say technological intervention should never be a matter of routine and that we don't know what subtle effect ultrasound might have on foetuses.

Routine scanning is expensive, upwards of £20 million a year in Britain. In Australia, more is spent on scanning than on the rest of maternity care put together. No data is kept on women and babies exposed to it and the World Health Organisation has issued a policy statement stressing that 'ultrasound screening during pregnancy is now in widespread use without sufficient evaluation'.

Pregnancy is a natural process, with uncertainties that no medical care can eliminate. An ecological approach does everything possible to keep mother and baby healthy while avoiding medical interference. Ultrasound should be used when necessary, not routinely.

Natural Birth

Parents-to-be are vulnerable to pressure from those who are providing antenatal care. One of the ways the medical profession took control of maternal services was to make birth a hospital procedure. In 1970, a government report recommended that all births should take place in hospital, and the trend towards hospital confinements which started early in the century has continued, from a total of 90 per cent of babies born in hospital at that time to 99 per cent in the mid-eighties. (Home births are now slightly on the increase.) The notion that hospital births are safer than births in small GP units or at home was uncontested until statistician Marjorie Tew found that the presumed connection between hospital births and reduced infant mortality did not exist and that home birth is statistically safer, in every risk category. A woman who has a home birth is continually told how brave she must be, but those of us who have done it often feel that it is having a hospital birth that requires bravery!

There are a number of organisations which will help you if you want to have a home birth. Community midwives are obliged by law to attend any birth in their area and the presence of a supportive spouse or midwife during labour does more than technological management to reduce the need for Caesarean and forceps deliveries.

In hospital you are far more likely to end up with what is euphemistically called a 'managed labour' – with electronic foetal monitoring, artificial breaking of the waters and the use of hormones to speed labour. Hospital routine makes a timetable for labour more likely, and the simple fact that equipment, drugs and staff are available make it more likely that they will be used. There is also an apt expression, the 'cascade of management', used to describe the way one act of intervention leads to another (if a woman has an anaesthetic, for example, she is more likely to need a forceps delivery). The most important factor in a successful labour is that the woman feels at ease in her surroundings and confident about her own ability to give birth.

Breastfeeding

There are many reasons to breastfeed. Babies raised on mother's milk are generally healthier and less likely to have allergies in later life, while women who breastfeed are less likely to contract breast cancer. Scandals about the selling of artificial milk products to women in the Third World, with advertising to persuade them that 'formula' is superior to their breastmilk, have had considerable press coverage. But only 64 per cent of British mothers choose to breastfeed their babies and of that number, only 40 per cent (26 per cent of the total) continue to breastfeed for at least four months, the minimum period recommended by most paediatricians. A recent survey showed a slight decline in the number of breastfeeding mothers over the past decade.

One reason for this is that although breastfeeding is officially encouraged through the government's Breast is Best campaign, not nearly enough is done to make it easy for many new mothers. Midwives and nurses try to help, but hospital routine doesn't make early breastfeeding easy. (Having your baby at home does make breastfeeding easier in the early days; a domino scheme, where the mother and baby return home a few hours after birth, is also helpful.)

Surveys in the developing world suggest that no more than 1 per cent of rural women and 5 per cent of urban women are unable to nurse their babies. Yet many of us give up nursing because we haven't got enough milk. How can this be? The main problem is extremely simple: not allowing the baby to nurse enough. You also need to eat well and get enough rest. Take your cues from the baby and your own feelings. Many babies like to nurse on and off throughout the day (and night). The National Childbirth Trust trains breastfeeding counsellors who are knowledgeable, friendly and supportive. Do contact them if you need help.

Q Breastfeeding is easier if you take the baby to bed. A family bed is a happy option for some – a low bed or futon makes it easy. *(See Resources for more information.)*

Women who will comfortably bare their breasts on a beach can be shy about feeding a baby, no matter how discreetly. We so rarely see a mother breastfeeding that it doesn't seem normal or ordinary and any use of our breasts is treated as something sexual. Support from friends and family – female and male – is terribly important.

Nappies

When you have a leaky little one you get obsessed with nappies. Fathers swap notes on the best type and friends report on which shop has your favourite brand at 50p off. Of course I'm talking about disposable plastic-and-paper nappies, not the terry nappies our mothers or grandmothers boiled in a copper.

Sixty-five per cent of babies are now put into disposable

nappies and approximately nine million are used and discarded every day in Britain. Discarded, but unfortunately not disposed of. Disposable nappies simply are *not* disposable. They are non-degradable, a potential health hazard and they contribute to the depletion of limited timber and petroleum reserves.

Q It is estimated that 4 per cent of household solid waste is made up of soiled nappies. For every £1 we spend on disposable nappies, taxpayers will spend 10p on disposal.

The basis of modern sanitation is the separation of sewage from other rubbish, so it can be appropriately and safely treated. But thanks to disposable nappies, huge amounts of faecal matter are treated as part of the household rubbish and may be yet another source of groundwater contamination from landfill sites. In some US states, there are laws banning the deposit of human waste in the disposal stream – this is meant to apply to campers but ought also to apply to baby waste. Viruses from human faeces (including live vaccines from routine childhood immunisations) can leak into the earth and pollute underground water supplies.

'Keeps baby drier' actually means that his blanket or your knee is kept dry, while the moisture is sealed inside the disposable nappy, next to baby's skin. Nappy rash was virtually unknown before plastic pants became common in the 1950s, and the mother whose child has a recurrently raw and painful bottom will know that it is essential to get the baby out of 'ordinary', i.e. disposable, nappies. In such cases doctors suggest leaving babies bare as much as possible and at least temporarily switching to cloth nappies.

In spite of all this, I understand why people use disposables and I have used them myself. After all, everyone else seems to, including the maternity ward at your local hospital. This tacit medical endorsement, fortified by the free samples given to new mothers, is enough to convince many parents that disposables are the correct thing to use. Because they save time and effort they can seem worth the expense, though it is considerable: some

£1,500 for a child potty-trained by age two and a half. Although the initial expense of using cloth nappies and covers is much greater than buying a bag of disposables at the supermarket, in the long run this cuts costs by about half, even taking laundering into account, and subsequent babies add nothing to the total.

With modern washing machines and dryers, using cloth nappies is easy.

One reader suggests plumbing a tap next to the toilet for a short length of garden hose with a garden sprayer. He quickly sprays solid mess into the toilet and says this makes washing cloth nappies at home a breeze.

If, however, you do not wish to do the washing yourself, you could use a nappy service. Enterprising women have started these all over the country and the National Association of Nappy Services can help you find one *(see Resources)*. A nappy service provides cloth nappies and regular pick up and collection. You hand over your bucket of rinsed nappies and in return get a pile of bouncy fresh ones, washed and dried in high-temperature machines. The cost falls midway between washing your own and using disposables.

Cloth Nappy Checklist

Here is a checklist to help you make the most of using cloth nappies:

- Traditional terry nappies are very absorbent, but the large squares can be awkward. The new fitted ones, with shaped nylon covers, are easier to use. There are dozens of options and your local nappy service can help you choose.
- Make sure you have enough nappies – three to four dozen. You will also need water-resistant covers and a covered bucket to hold rinsed nappies.
- Keep the bucket near the loo. Half fill it with water and add a tablespoonful of borax or washing soda to reduce odours and staining.

- Wet nappies can go straight into the nappy bucket and soiled ones should be rinsed in the toilet bowl and placed in the bucket.
- When the nappies are ready to wash, drain the excess solution into the toilet, then use a spin cycle to drain dirty water. Then use a hot wash and double rinse.
- Do not use fabric softeners, which makes fabric less absorbent.
- Inside, you may want to use a tumbledryer on high heat to help sterilisation. Tumbling also makes the nappies softer than drying on a rack, but drying outside uses no energy and sunlight acts as a natural disinfectant and gentle bleach.
- Let your baby go bare whenever you can, inside and out.
- Don't feel guilty about using a disposable occasionally. But please don't use those scented plastic bags made to wrap disposables for disposal!

TIPS: FOR BABY CARE

- Ecologically speaking, the best baby wear has been worn before. Jumble sales have terrific bargains and if you're lucky friends and relatives may give you plenty to outfit your baby for the first year or two.
- Check your NCT branch newsletter, local free sheet and the notices in the newsagent's window or place your own advertisement for second-hand baby clothes.
- Sign up with a nappy service or buy three to four dozen cloth nappies and covers.
- Choose toys that are not made from soft plastics (see page 197).
- Buy a couple of good quality nursing bras – get advice from the NCT – and have support to hand for your first few days of breastfeeding.
- Stock up on non-toxic cleaning products, and follow the tips in Chapter 8 on hygiene so your baby doesn't grow up surrounded by dangerous fumes from household disinfectants.

17

Looking after your Family

Our children are growing up in a new century, with global opportunities, unprecedented information and surging technologies. We have to prepare them for their new world. How, in a consumerist world surrounded by advertising, can we encourage kids to value the natural world and care for one another? Many parents worry about violence on television. Some of us wonder how television watching and computer use is affecting children's academic performance and their ability to form relationships. This chapter surveys some important aspects of looking after your family: (1) health concerns, including diet, allergies and immunisation; (2) play and active games; (3) the effects of the media.

Health

Children are at more risk than adults from a wide range of environmental hazards. They are especially susceptible to certain chemical and radioactive hazards because they are developing rapidly. In addition, kids are disproportionately exposed to certain hazards because of their body weight and lung capacity, because they are nearer to the ground and because they put things into their mouths.

Our kids spend one quarter of their time in school buildings. Newer buildings can present the same health problems as office blocks, especially if ventilation is inadequate. A group of active children confined in a closed room for hours can lead to air quality worse than that in a submarine!

Many parents are unaware that pesticides, as well as toxic cleaning products, are used in and around schools on a routine basis. For the most part, school authorities have given little attention to the role such exposure could have on students' learning ability and intellectual development. In the years ahead, we can expect to see more attention given to effects of environmental factors such as air quality and natural daylight on student behaviour and academic performance.

But don't try to keep your child or home *too* clean. Children exposed to everyday bacteria, garden soil, woodlands and animals are less likely to develop allergies. There are some pathogens to worry about, though, and hand washing after using the loo and before eating is most important *(see also Chapter 1)*.

>Toxic Toys

Toxic additives called phthalates are used to soften vinyl in toys, IV-fluid bags and for many other consumer uses. Global companies are following through on commitments to eliminate vinyl products entirely, but in the meantime, try to eliminate soft plastics, known as polyvinyl chloride or PVC, from your child's life.

Greenpeace has led an international campaign against toxic toys and especially against the use of phthalates in teething toys designed for children under three. Phthlates are thought to damage organs and interfere with sperm production. If you can smell a plastic, avoid it and make sure it doesn't contaminate your home environment.

>Immunisation

Most health-care professionals insist that immunisation is both safe and necessary. Even teenagers are now being immunised against meningitis and hepatitis, and of course adults get immunised before travelling to certain parts of the world. The eradication of smallpox and near eradication of polio are credits to immunisation programmes, but many common childhood diseases were already in decline before many modern vaccines thanks to better hygiene, clean water and an improved diet.

Some critics of routine vaccination claim that the system gives parents a sense of false security and doesn't allow children's immune system to cope with routine diseases in a way appropriate and necessary for lifelong good health. Others see a relationship between the increase in asthma, air pollution and vaccination.

While reassuring the public that all is well with current immunisation programmes, the medical profession and governments are looking for alternatives. A new whooping cough vaccine which does not seem to have the same worrying side effects – which can include seizures and other severe reactions – is being tested in the United States and Sweden.

If you have a young baby, take the time to look into the question of immunisation before you make up your mind. Your GP or health visitor will press you to have the baby's first set of shots at two months, but the timing is not crucial; if you're uncertain, take time to understand fully the pros and cons.

>Fluoride

Until the 1930s, fluoride was considered a poison and its disposal was a problem for the expanding steel and aluminium industries. At the same time, the sugar industry wanted to find a way of reducing tooth decay without lowering sugar consumption. Small amounts of fluoride had this effect (in large doses, fluoride causes mottling, brittle teeth and abnormal bone formation). The aluminium and steel industries were eventually able to sell their waste to water authorities to fluoridate water supplies and an enormous amount of toxic waste could be disposed of.

The fluoridation of water has been much criticised as

involuntary mass medication. Proper brushing habits and a nutritious diet low in sugar should be the basis of dental health. If necessary, children can take fluoride drops in a prescribed dose rather than rely on random intake from toothpaste or tap water.

>Lice

Environmentalists suspect that the current resurgence of lice is the result of the overuse of pesticides, which have encouraged the creepy-crawlies to mutate into ever more resistant forms. Certainly 'treatment failure' is now common and experts agree that the most, perhaps the only, completely reliable method of removal is thorough combing. While we don't like having intimate contact with insects, excessively strong pesticide solutions and shampoos are not a good long-term solution. Be alert to scratching and make weekly head checks just in case. The earlier lice are spotted, the easier they are to deal with. Read shampoo labels and choose those which are pyrethrum-based; avoid lindane altogether.

Environmental specialists recommend coconut oil-based shampoos to kill lice and in my experience this works well. Other natural remedies are rosemary and lavender essential oils, and a tea made from quassia chips. In any case, careful combing (under bright light) and daily screening is still necessary. Get a metal lice comb, not the plastic kind that comes with shampoos.

>A Child's Diet

Recent analyses of schoolchildren's diets have shown startling cases of malnourishment. British children not only eat far too much sugar and fat, but are short of major quantifiable nutrients. They are spending more than £220 million a year on sweets and snacks on their way to and from secondary schools, and have developed eating habits based on grazing quick-fix snacks with little nutritive content. Breaking the fast-food habit – or not letting it get started – will set your children on the path to eco eating and good health.

Here are some general guidelines for eating with children:

- Let your child join in with your meals from about six months, with tiny tastes of suitable foods.
- Introduce a wide variety of foods, both cooked and raw.
- Never force food on a child and don't panic if your child doesn't eat as much as you think he should.
- Aim for a balanced diet over the course of each week, not each day.
- Don't let a child who isn't eating meals have sweets and crisps.
- Notice which nutritious foods your children like and try to emphasise those dishes.
- Kids love to cook – let them get involved in meal planning and preparation as early as possible.
- They also love tastings, especially with blindfolds and score cards. Taste different jams, milks and butters and advance to olive oils and cheeses.

Play and Relationships

The ability to develop close relationships in later life is closely linked to childhood friendships. Some studies suggest that other children are even more important than the mother in a child's emotional development. Children need to spend informal time together, not only school time or organised visits.

A dependence on toys has a lot to do with not having enough companionship. Nowadays even babies have cupboards full of battery-driven stuffed dogs and helicopters with revolving blades, and good old Lego comes with ready-made detail. These toys are designed for what one box describes as 'imaginative play' – that is, play the way the designer imagines it, not play which genuinely encourages a child's imagination. How a child copes with this depends on her own independence and self-confidence, and on whether her parents too feel the need to have every new gadget.

The environmental and social consequences of this are profound. The sheer quantity of raw materials used to make toys (most of which don't last for long) is one aspect of the problem. Even more important are the lessons children learn about ceaseless consumption, ready-made entertainment and disposability.

Toys shouldn't be substitutes for hands-on assistance from parents. Often a child just needs a little adult aid to turn a cardboard box into a spaceship or a sturdy fruit crate into a cooker.

Let children join in your tasks whenever you can – it's good for them to feel that they can help. They can also acquire useful skills early in life (sewing on buttons may seem great fun to an eight year old).

TIPS: FOR TOYS

- Choose toys made of natural materials: cloth, paper, leather, natural fleece, wood *(Good Wood, of course; see pages 109–10)* and metal.
- Buy for durability. Toys made of solid natural materials are expensive, but they can be passed to friends, sold through small ads or saved for the grandchildren.
- Borrowed or jumble sale or toys are great and my kids enjoy buying directly from other children at boot fairs.
- Toy libraries will give your children a great deal of variety and save you money.
- Let children play with real things: put together a child-sized collection of pots and pans and dishes, instead of a tiny plastic kitchen.
- A dressing-up box is essential: children love long, sparkly, over-the-top clothes and funny shoes and hats.
- A button box, handy for sewing and mending, can be a treasure trove. So can a collection of seashells.
- Stick with pencils, chalk and crayons, instead of plastic pens or marking pens that contain chemical solvents.

- Let children use the back of printed sheets of paper to draw on, or buy drawing pads made of recycled paper. Blackboards and writing slates are fun too.
- A Wendy house is an excellent way to use scrap wood, mouldings, carpet and wallpaper.
- Charades is a great game to play with kids of all ages. It's terrific fun and also draws on verbal skills and lateral thinking.
- Climbing trees is important to kids, so try to find somewhere where it's OK for them to climb.
- Wild places are also significant in children's psyches. Maybe you can holiday in a place where your children can build forts or make a leafy cave. Gardens can also be planned to allow for childhood hideaways.

>Quality Time

Children aren't born with a fully wired brain. Many aspects of brain function are literally programmed by experience as an infant and small child. Psychologists and those in education are trying to work out why children today have more trouble concentrating at school, why they don't read and why they are so easily distracted. The easy answer is: 'Television.' The more complex answer is that our lifestyles have changed in ways that seem to be affecting children's mental and emotional development.

The main premise of eco living is that we need to find ways to live in harmony with the demands of nature – with our own nature as well as that of the natural world. It seems that our lifestyles are not giving children what they need to mature properly in terms of cognitive or physical development, and some would claim that today's loose social structures do not offer what they need for healthy emotional development either.

Technology cannot guide our children's development and in fact probably hinders it. Many things that have been part of child rearing in every culture are missing from ours. Children spend less time playing or listening to or conversing with others and they are indoors far more. They do not learn practical skills by observing or working with adults.

Too much noise and over-programming prevents children from developing what psychologists call 'inner speech' – the internal control mechanisms that help them make choices and regulate their own behaviour. Effective inner speech develops from the earliest interactions between infant and caregiver, as the child learns ways of affecting the world outside. As the child grows, he learns to evaluate and talk through problems – how to cross the road or wait his turn or dispose of a plastic wrapper. Talking to children and encouraging them to talk back is crucial in this process.

'Quality time' is a phantom concept. For children, there is only time. They need, first and foremost, to spend lots of time with adults, watching the adult process information and make decisions. New trends in the workplace, towards flexible hours and telecommuting, may help both mothers and fathers, and extended family members, to arrange their lives to allow a more balanced family life. (For more on this topic, I recommend a book called *Endangered Minds; see Bibliography*.)

>Celebrations

Another lifestyle issue affecting our kids is a lack of clear routines and family involvement. Kids learn from daily and weekly routines, and it's important to provide this kind of certainty wherever you can. It's even more important to articulate the routines, for example: 'Now we lay the table. We need forks and knives and glasses.'

Besides these routines, rituals and celebrations encourage a child to recognise longer periods of time, anticipate pleasures and participate in creating something beautiful. Many religious rituals – the Friday evening shabbat candles or dressing for church on Sunday morning – offer this. You can create your own small rituals, even something as simple as arranging the first daffodils of spring in a pretty jar.

>Staying Active

Active children are more alert, better tempered and healthier. They will become active adults with less chance of developing heart disease, osteoporosis and other ailments. But modern children are far less active than their parents or grandparents were, and the health effects are obvious. Obesity has risen dramatically and general fitness levels are poor.

Experts recommend at least an hour a day of vigorous activity, and walking or cycling to school is one way to start. Transport 2000 is working with schools on school travel schemes that emphasise walking and cycling. Don't let the thought of pollution deter you – a child riding inside a car on a busy road is exposed to more pollution than a child walking. If you walk, too, you can help your child develop good pedestrian skills and the confidence to travel alone later on.

It's important to get pre-school children walking, too. Take your child out of the pushchair and walk hand in hand so you can talk, look into each other's faces, examine leaves and converse with a squirrel! After-school physical activities are important as well. Tree climbing, cycling, active games and garden chores develop muscles and motor skills. Kids also need adult models. It's great fun to get involved in the games or sports your child enjoys – when did you last kick a football or swing a bat? – or to try something new together – my son and I are learning to rock climb.

TIPS: FOR ENJOYING TIME WITH YOUR CHILD

- Learn the art of storytelling.
- Read aloud together.
- Make music and listen to music.
- Get busy with crafts and projects.
- Relish the 'whys' – it's the most important question there is.
- Explore the world around you together.
- Dig the garden.

The Media

>Television

Current studies of television viewing associate it with short attention span, lack of 'reflectiveness' (the ability to think), poor logical ability and atrophy of the imagination. Children raised on television often do not know how to play – they simply imitate characters and situations they've seen on the telly. Television violence creates a climate of social 'dis-ease', a feeling that the world outside is a dangerous place, and much TV exposes tiny children to an onslaught of advertising. In addition, there is persuasive evidence that television watching is a significant factor in failure at school.

Think about getting rid of the television, or drastically restricting its presence in your home, especially while your children are very young. Children should be playing with other kids or running around outside, not watching cartoons.

There's a common notion that if kids aren't watching TV they will be bothering adults. First, children throughout the millennia have amused themselves. They can make toys from sticks and bits of paper, or watch a fly – *if* they have been encouraged to do so. And they can and should be involved in adult activities whenever possible. It's easier to do the washing up yourself, but a child learns important things from working with an adult: 'Let's see, we need a capful of washing-up liquid and a tea towel. Is this dish clean or should we wash it again?' This processing teaches planning and self-control.

>Computer Games and the Internet

Use of the Internet for school projects is one thing – though even here children should be learning to assess the sources and quality of information – but online recreation is quite another thing. All the developmental issues discussed above, from physical fitness to social skills, are influenced by time spent in front of the computer. It worries me that my son wants to play online computer games against a friend who lives nearby. I encourage them to be outside playing basketball or exploring the woods instead.

Watching TV or playing computer games together is not, in psychological terms, social interaction and the sheer number of hours that can be absorbed by these activities is a problem in itself. No other human activity – planting trees, cooking or making love – can be done for such huge amounts of time. This suggests a numbing quality which isn't what we want for our children. Little research has been done on the social and psychological consequences of Internet use, but what there is suggests a link between depression and computer time. What counts, for adults and children, is what Elizabeth Barrett Browning called 'fellowship and social comfort' – time with real people, solving real problems and enjoying the glorious, complicated real world we live in.

Learning

Access to good education is fundamental to any democratic society and the information and attitudes that today's children acquire at school will affect the future for all of us.

Schools have traditionally served a social function in communities, for parents as well as children. Local schools are an important factor in neighbourhood or village life, and many studies show that small schools produce better results.

Awareness of nature and of environmental problems is one of the things we want to teach our children and schools are now doing more to help. You can be involved, too, by encouraging your child's delight in the outdoors ('Feel the rain on your face!'), care for others and the environment ('Let's put this bit of paper in the recycling bin') and, most importantly, by encouraging a sense of wonder at nature.

Talk about what you know and want to know (looking something up with a child is a lesson for both of you). Explain why you are choosing organic apples instead of the shiny red ones in the big pile and exclaim about the beauties you see around you, too – it's vital to talk about good things as well as bad. I got the idea for my children's book *Rachel's Roses* when my daughter got upset because I put some dead flowers onto the compost pile. I had to explain to her about the cycles of nature and how new flowers would grow from the compost we made. Nature is exciting to children and we can all learn from the questions they ask: 'Why do people drive so much? Where does the dirty water go?'

Afterword

We can change the world together, by doing things differently ourselves and pushing companies and governments to go about their business in new ways. We can make practical choices that will create stronger families and communities while enabling us to enjoy a world that is indeed threatened but is still resilient and beautiful.

Individual action isn't everything. We need to support one another. It's energising to get together with other people to work on a cause you care about, whether it's getting your university to buy recycled paper or working with your council on a pedestrian scheme. The Resources section which follows will help with further information and contacts.

One mistake made by the politically active is always campaigning *against* things. They can give an impression of being negative, trying to curtail other people's freedom – or just keep them from having fun! It's time to reframe the debate, promoting a vision of a sustainable world and sustainable values. A project to get kids walking and cycling to school (*see Transport 2000, page 214*), for example, is about improving health, encouraging parents and caregivers to walk with kids and breaking down the isolation created by a car-oriented culture. Here, to start you thinking about your own vision, is a short manifesto for living lightly.

Walk It

My brother Dan was in Delta Force, an élite unit of the US Green Berets. When I began to write about the environment, he asked, 'Do you talk the walk or walk the talk?' That is, do you swagger and show off, or really do the job?

It's vital to walk the talk, even when it takes a little extra effort. You can set an example in little ways, at home and at work, by turning down the heating or choosing organic milk. And you can set an example in big ways, too, now and then. Switch your company to post-consumer recycled paper for all its corporate printing and annual reports, or give up a second car, or install solar panels when you renovate your house.

Familiarise yourself with the background to a few issues or causes – perhaps by refreshing your school chemistry or doing some historical research on local industry or taking an evening course in nutrition – to become more confident, and more effective, as an eco-activist.

Talk It

Talk does count as well. You can make a difference by telling people why you're doing what you do. Talk to them about the issues that concern you.

You can telephone or write to organisations about their policies. Companies and elected officials get nervous when their customers and constituents start to complain. Several major companies, including McDonald's and Shell, have made huge public relations gaffes in recent years by ignoring consumers' reasonable concerns about the environmental impact of what they do.

I'm sceptical about those little printed cards that some green organisations encourage us to send out. Writing a few sincere and serious letters is going to have more impact than stamping dozens of prepared cards, and it's more satisfying too. Exercise your creative talents by expressing why a politician's position offends you and tell companies what you think they should do. Think about whom you're writing to. What will make them listen to you? If you think you represent others – your neighbours, other mothers you've spoken to – say so. If you're a regular customer or have special expertise, tell them. It's fine to write regular letters to your representatives in local or national government, but make sure you write about substantial and relevant issues.

Work It

While most of us need a job to put a roof over our heads, the work we do provides us with far more than just a monthly bank deposit. It can wreck a mood or a marriage and in the long term it's going to affect how we feel about our lives and the impact we've made on the world.

More and more of us are looking for work that has meaning and you can choose a career that makes a difference. That doesn't necessarily mean working for Greenpeace or VSO (though you may want to shimmy up a tanker or teach English in an African village). There are a huge range of careers – from environmental law to eco product design – to consider.

Whatever you do, try to do good at work. It doesn't matter if you work on a shopfloor or as a banker, there are always opportunities to green your workplace in some way or chat over eco news with co-workers. More important, think about moving within your field towards a speciality that will allow you to earn a living and do good at the same time.

Invest It

If you don't approve of something, you can refuse to buy it and write to the manufacturer to explain why. You can send donations to environmental charities that support education programmes and campaigns, or help young organic farmers get a start. You can also encourage good business practice through ethical investing.

Conventional investment strategies are based on the assumption that people want the maximum returns without regard for social or environmental costs. But an increasing number of investors want to make informed financial decisions, put their money behind the causes they care about and refuse to endorse corporate irresponsibility. *Which?* magazine's analysis has found that ethical funds perform overall at least as well as unvetted unit trusts and there are now dozens of ethical and green funds to choose from.

Business people sometimes seem to take environmental concerns more seriously than do politicians, as they have to think ahead, considering future markets, possible lawsuits and ways to strengthen the overall performance of their company. Encourage them to do better by investing in companies whose performance is good and encourage companies to sign the CERES Principles (a set of corporate principles to minimise pollution and waste, conserve energy, offer safe products and services, and use natural resources in a sustainable manner). *(For further information, contact one of the umbrella organisations listed in the Resources section.)*

LETS!

A growing trend is the setting up of local exchange trading schemes (LETS), a sophisticated form of barter that enables people to make purchases and be paid for their services or products, from calligraphy to cakes, in a variety of different units, such as Olivers (Bath) or Solents (Southampton) rather than in pounds sterling.

The concept of LETS developed in Canada in the eighties and has spread around the world. There are hundreds of local schemes in Britain and the idea is spreading. Records are maintained by a management group and statements and directories of services are sent out periodically. The schemes benefit people who have skills or products but no job or market outlet within the national economy, and they make regions less dependent on outside employment and markets. They also enable people to make greater use of their skills and, naturally, strengthen ties between neighbours. *(See Resources for more information.)*

Finally, Reach Out

It's harder and harder, especially if you live in a city, to keep the environment from becoming an abstraction. Office blocks are window-less and you may rush from bus to Underground with nary a glance at the sky. But it's important to find ways to stay in touch with the world. Watch the seasons. Take time to touch the bark of a tree or listen to birdsong.

Reach out, too, to other people. It's easy to write an annual cheque or fill in a standing order form to the environmental groups of your choice. What's more difficult is getting involved in a personal way. But in this increasingly fragmented and technologically driven time, we need to revalue our human contacts and get to know the natural world, as well. Empowerment comes from hands-on involvement.

Don't try to turn your life upside-down and don't feel guilty because you continue to drive your children to music lessons, but keep looking for options and evaluating your choices.

We're in this together – write and tell me how you're doing! *(You can reach me at karen@berkshirereference.com, or c/o the publishers. For more information visit www.iEcoLiving.com.)*

KC, 17 April 2000

Bibliography

Ballantine, Richard and Grant, Richard, *DK Living: Ultimate Bicycle Book,* Dorling Kindersley, 1998

Barnes, Belinda and Gail Bradley, Suzanne, *Planning for a Healthy Baby,* Vermilion, 1994

Bender Birch, Beryl, *Power Yoga,* Prion Books, 1995

Body Shop Book of Well Being, The, Ebury Press, 1998

Brown, Lester, *The State of the World: 2000,* Earthscan, 2000

Burke, David and Lotus, Jean, *Get a Life!,* Bloomsbury, 2000

Carey, Diana and Large, Judy, *Festivals, Family and Food,* Hawthorn Press, 1982

Elkington, John and Hailes, Julia, *The New Foods Guide,* Gollancz, 1999

Elkington, John and Hailes, Julia, *Manual 2000,* Hodder & Stoughton, 1998

Fisher, Jeffrey A., *The Plague Makers,* Simon & Schuster, 1994

Harland, Edward, *Eco-Renovation,* Resurgence Books, 1994

Harper, Peter *et al, The Natural Garden Book,* Gaia Books, 1994

Healey, Jane M., *Endangered Minds: Why children don't think and what we can do about it,* Touchstone, Simon & Schuster, 1999

Healey, Jane M. , *Failure to Comment,* Pocket Books, 2000

Jackson, Deborah, *Three in a Bed,* Bloomsbury, 1999

Kitzinger , Sheila, *The New Pregnancy and Childbirth,* Penguin Books, 1997

Kowalchik, Claire, *The Complete Book of Running for Women,* Pocket Books, 1999

La Leche League, *The Art of Breastfeeding,* available from La Leche League or The National Childbirth Trust

Lang, Peter, *LETS Work: Rebuilding the local economy*. This and other hard to obtain books, as well as some truly alternative books, are available from Eco-logic Books, Mulberry House, 19 Maple Grove, Bath, BA2 3AF; Tel: 01225 484472, Fax: 0117 942 0164.

Larkcom, Joy, *The Salad Garden,* F. Lincoln, 1994

Lazarus, Pat, *Keep Your Pet Healthy the Natural Way,* Fawcett Crest, 1999

Levy, Stuart B., *The Antibiotic Paradox: How miracle drugs are destroying the miracle,* Plenum Publishing, 1992

Lobstein, Tim, *Children's Food,* Unwin Hyman, 1998; available from The Food Commission

Mabey, Richard, *Food for Free,* Collins, 1972

Mabey, Richard, *Plants with a Purpose*, Collins, 1977

Mabey, Richard, *Flora Britannica*, Sinclair Stevenson, 1996

Miller, Neil Z., *Immunization Theory vs. Reality: Exposé on vaccinations,* New Atlantean Press, 1995

O'Mara, Peggy, ed., 'Vaccination: The issue of our times', *Mothering,* Santa Fe, New Mexico, 1997

Obolensky, Kira, *The Not So Big House: A blueprint for the way we really live,* Taunton Press, 1998

Pears, Pauline and Strickland, Sue, *Organic Gardening,* Mitchell Beazley, 1999

Pearson, David, *The Natural House Book,* Conran Octopus, 1994

Rifkin, Jeremy, *The Biotech Century,* Phoenix Press,1999

Lynn Robinson and Gordon Thomson, *Body Control the Pilates Way,* Pan, 1998

Vale, Brenda and Robert, *The New Autonomous House,* Thames and Hudson, 2000

Wildwood, Chrissie, *Encyclopedia of Healing Plants: A complete guide to aromatherapy, flower essences and herbal remedies,* Piatkus, 1999

Resources

The Bates Association for Vision Education
PO Box 25, Shoreham-by-Sea, W. Sussex BN43
Tel: 01273 422090; Fax: 01273 179983
Website: www.seeing.org

Buy Recycled
National Recycling Forum/Waste Watch
Europa House, 13–7 Ironmonger Row, London EC1V 3QN
Tel: 020 7253 6266; Fax: 020 7253 5962
Website: www.nrf.org.uk
Publishes a listing of produces containing recycled materials and over
1,000 recycled products.

The Centre for Alternative Technology
Llwyngwern Quarry, Machynlleth, Powys, SY20 9AZ
Tel: 01654 702400
Website: www.cat.org.uk
Exhibitions and displays open to visitors; weekend courses. Send
£1.30 in stamps for their mail order book list.

Common Ground
PO Box 25309, London NW5 1ZA
Tel: 020 7267 2144
Charity working to conserve nature, landscape and place with the
help of those in the arts.

Eco Living

The Consumers' Association
2 Marylebone Road, London NW1 4DF
Tel: 020 7486 5544
Website: www.which.net
The Consumers' Association publications, such as *Which?*, frequently cover green consumer issues.

Dr Hadwen Trust
FREEPOST SG335, Hitchin, Herts., SG5 2BR
Tel: 01462 436819; Fax: 01462 436844
Website: www.drhadwentrust.org.uk
Conducts research into alternatives to the use of animals in research and testing.

The Earth Centre
Doncaster
Tel: 01709 513933
Website: www.earthcentre.org.uk
A recreational centre funded by the Millennium Fund to showcase environmental initiatives and educational programmes.

The Ecology Building Society
18 Station Road, Crosshills, Keighley, West Yorkshire, BD20 8TB
Tel: 01535 635933
Website: www.ecology.co.uk

English Nature
Northminster House, Peterborough, PE1 1UA
Tel: 01733 455000; Fax: 01733 568834
Website: www.english-nature.org.uk
Statutory services responsible for looking after England's wild plants and animals.

The Environmental and Energy Awareness Division, Department of the Environment, Transport and the Regions
123 Victoria Street, London SW1E 6OE
Tel: 020 7890 6696
Website: www.environment.detr.gov.uk/index.htm
Offers governmental reports on a wide variety of green issues, useful if you want to get some background from a source other than campaigning organisations or companies.

Environmental Health
The environmental health department of your local council should be able to give you advice on asbestos, lead in paint, radon, chemical safety (such as pesticide spraying in parks) and the proper disposal of hazardous chemicals.

The Environmental Transport Association
10 Church Street, Weybridge, KT13 8RS
Tel: 01932 828882
Website: www.eta.co.uk
Provider of car and bicycle (yes, really!) breakdown services while campaigning for environmentally sound transport.

Ethical Consumer magazine
ECRA Publishing, FREEPOST NWW978A, Manchester M15 9EP
Tel: 0161 226 2929
Website: www.ethicalconsumer.org
Provides news on corporate campaigning, consumer boycotts, ethical investment, organic food and green issues and products.

The Ethical Investment Group
Greenfield House, Guiting Power, Cheltenham, GL54 5TZ
Tel: 01242 604550
Website: www.oneworld.org/ethical-investors
Independent financial advisers on ethical investments. Half of their profits goes to charity.

Ethical Investment Services
33 Ribblesdale Place, Preston, Lancashire, PR1 3NA
Tel: 0800 018 8557
Provides advice on ethical investment. Call for a free copy of *The Ethical Investment Association's Guide to Ethical Investment* by John Fleetwood.

The Food Commission
94 White Lion Street. London N1 9PF
Tel: 020 7837 2250
E-mail: foodcomm@compuserve.com
Some excellent publications on healthy eating are available, including the *Food* magazine.

Foresight
28 The Paddock, Godalming, Surrey, GU7 1XD
Tel: 01483 427839
An organisation devoted to pre-natal care. Send a SAE for information on courses, membership and free leaflet, *Preparing for Pregnancy*.

Forest Stewardship Council
1134 29th Street NW, Washington, DC 20007
Tel: (+1) 877 372 5646 (toll free); Fax: (+1) 202 342 6589
Sets standards for wood certification in conjunction with the World Wide Fund for Nature.

Friends of the Earth
26–28 Underwood Street, London N1 7JQ
Tel: 020 7490 1555
Website: www.foe.co.uk
FoE's range of publications is considerable and includes excellent teaching packs for schools.

The Genetic Engineering Network (GEN)
PO Box 9656, London N4 4YJ
Tel: 020 8374 9516
Website: www.dmac.co.uk/gen.html
Acts a clearinghouse for genetic engineering information for the public.

The Genetics Forum
94 White Lion Street, London N1 9PF
Tel: 020 7837 9229
Website: www.geneticsforum.org.uk
Concerned with the health and environmental risks of genetic technologies and their ethical implications.

Global Action Plan (GAP)
9 Fulwood Place, London WC1V 6HG
Tel: 020 7405 5633
Develops programmes of activity for people to take practical environmental action in their homes, at work and in the community. Contact GAP for an information pack.

Going for Green
Elizabeth House, The Pier, Wigan, WN3 4EX
Tel: 01942 612621
Website: www.gfg.iclnet.co.uk
Britain's largest environmental awareness campaign. Get in touch for information on their five-point Green Code and action pack.

GreenNet
4th Floor, 393–395 City Road, London EC1V 1NE
Tel: 020 7713 1941
Website: www.gn.apc.org
Part of an international network which links environmental, peace and social justice groups and interested individuals.

Hammett Recycled Stationery
Steve and Susan Hammett, Gate Farm, Fen End, Kenilworth, Warwickshire, CV8 1NW
Tel: 01676 533832
Website: www.ourworld.compuserve.com/homepage/hammett
A noteworthy source of personal and business stationery, design and printing, and innovative paper products. Free catalogue. Send three first-class stamps for paper samples.

International Center for Technology Assessment
666 Pennsylvania Ave. SE, Suite 302
Washington, DC 20003
(+1) 202-547-9359 (phone)
(+1) 202-547-9429 (fax)
www.icta.org
Provides information to the general public and policy-makers on the economic, ethical, social, environmental and political impacts of new technologies.

The London Hazards Centre
Interchange Studios, Dalby Street, London NW5 3NQ
Tel: 020 7267 3397
Website: www.lhc.org.uk/contact.htm
Aims to help people prevent and combat hazards in their working lives and community. Publishes practical handbooks on health and safety.

Eco Living

Mailing Preference Service (also the Telephone Preference Service)
Reef House, Plantation Wharf, London SW11 3UF
Tel: 020 7738 9053; Fax 020 7978 4918
Write to Freepost 22, London W1E 7EZ or call 0345 034599 for an
application form. Enables any member of the public to have their
name deleted from or added to a mailing list. Sponsored by trade
associations and the Post Office, and considered by many to be
ineffectual. Try complaining to the Advertising Standards Authority
(www.asa.org.uk).

The National Association of Nappy Services (NANS)
St George House, Hill Street, Birmingham B5 4AN
Tel: 0121 693 4949
Call to find out how to contact your nearest nappy washing service.
See also The Real Nappy Association.

The National Childbirth Trust (NCT)
Alexandra House, Oldham Terrace, London W3 6NH
Tel: 020 8992 8637; Fax: 020 8992 5929
Website: www.nct-online.org/main.htm
Call or write for their publications list.

The National Federation of Women's Institutes (WI)
Public Affairs Department, 104 New Kings Road, London SW6 4LY
Tel: 020 7371 9300
Website: www.nfwi.org.uk
The WI has been active in developing ideas and programmes related
to Local Agenda 21, often with governmental and other
organisations, and has a distinct focus on progressive environmental
and community issues.

Natural Collection
PO Box 2111, Bath, BA1 2ZQ
Tel: 01225 442288; Fax: 01225 469673
A company which sells a great traditional clothes dryer and organic
cottons, but some silly stuff too.

The Natural Death Centre
20 Heber Road, London NW2 6AA
Tel: 020 8208 2853
Website: www.worldtrans.org/naturaldeath.html
The New Natural Death Handbook, which includes information on
the laws surrounding DIY burials, is available for £1.65.

Neal's Yard
26–34 Ingate Place, Battersea, London SW8 3NS
Tel: 020 7498 1686; Fax: 020 7498 2055
E-mail: mail@nealsyardremedies.com
A mail order source of pricey but wonderful skin and body care
products made with organic and completely natural ingredients.

The Organic Food Federation
The Tithe House, Peaseland Green, Elsing, East Dereham, Norfolk,
NR20 3DY
Tel: 01362 637314
Website: www.organicfood.co.uk/off/
Federal inspection agency as well as provider of information to the
public on growing organic foods.

The Organic Horticultural Association
National Centre for Organic Gardening, Ryton-on-Dunsmore,
Coventry, CV8 3LG
Tel: 01203 303517
Website: www.oha.org.uk
Membership includes a quarterly newsletter, free gardening advice
and unlimited entry to Ryton Gardens. Send off for their
publications list.

Original Organics
Unit 9, Langlands Business Park, Uffculme, Culloptom, Devon, EX15 3DA
Tel: 01884 841515
The Original Wormery and the Rotal Compost Converter are both
available from this company.

Eco Living

Permaculture magazine
Permanent Publications, Hyden House Limited, The Sustainability
Centre, East Meon, Hampshire, GU32 1HR
Tel: 01730 823311; Fax: 01730 823322
Website: www.permaculture.co.uk
Permaculture has taken on general coverage of green innovatives –
some counterculture and quite bizarre, some truly significant –
along with its central focus on a particular approach to food
production.

The Ramblers' Association
1–5 Wandsworth Road, London SW8 2XX
Tel: 020 7339 8500
Website: www.ramblers.org.uk/index.html
A membership organisation supporting ramblers' rights and
organising events and walking holidays.

The Real Nappy Association
PO Box 3704, London SE26 4RX. Tel: 020 8299 4519
Website: www.realnappy.com
For sources of mail order modern washable nappies and other advice,
and links to nappy services.

A Responsible Investment? A 2000 report available for £15.00 in
print online form from SustainAbility: A complete guide to socially
responsible investment (SRI), the selection of companies, new
indexes and rating systems for business, institutional and private
investors.
www.sustainability.co.uk

Resurgence magazine
Ford House, Hartland Bideford, Devon, EX39 6EE
Tel: 01273 441293; Fax: 1237 441203
Website: www.resurgence.org
The leading UK alternative magazine, with an international
perspective, published by the E. F. Schumacher Society.

The Royal Society for the Protection of Birds (RSPB)
The Lodge, Sandy, Bedfordshire, SG19 2DL
Tel: 01767 680551
Website: www.rspb.org.uk
Free leaflets covering all aspects of encouraging birds, from proper feeding to providing birdhouses. Enclose an SAE.

The SeaWeb
Website: www.seaweb.org
Helpful site that provides links to many useful and informative organisations which focus on preserving the ocean and informing the public of fish issues.

Slow Food International
via della Mendicit
Istruita 45
45-12042 Bra (Cuneo), Italy
fax: (+39) 0172 421293
phone: (+39) 0172 419611
Food lovers who enjoy leisurely, sociable eating and support artisan producers and organic farmers – call or email to join (or start) a local group, known as a Convivium.

The Soil Association
86 Colston Street, Bristol, BS1 5BB
Tel: 0117 929 0661
Website: www.soilassociation.org
Certifies farms and organically grown food. Write for *Where to Buy Organic* Food (£5) as well as much information on peat-free alternatives and other publications.

Suffolk Herbs
Monks Farm, Coggeshall Road, Kelvedon, Essex, CO5 9PG
Tel: 01376 572456; Fax: 01376 571189
Website: www.suffolkherbs.com
One of my favourite gardening catalogues, offering a wide range of herbs, salad greens, seeds and books.

Eco Living

SustainAbility
49–53 Kensington High Street, London W8 5ED
Tel: 020 7937 9996
Website: www.sustainability.co.uk
Business and green consumer publications and international business
consultancy, started by the authors of the *Green Consumer Guide*
and *New Foods Guide*.

Sustrans
35 King Street, Bristol BS1 4DZ
Tel: 0117 929 0888
Website: www.sustrans.org.uk
Sustrans – sustainable transportation – focuses on building a National
Cycle Network and Safe Routes to Schools.

Tourism Concern
Stapleton House, University of North London, 277–281 Holloway
Road, London N7 8HN
Tel: 020 7753 3330
Website: www.gn.apc.org/tourismconcern
Promotes the understanding of the impact of tourism on the
environment and on people living in holiday areas.

Transport 2000
The Impact Centre, 12–18 Hoxton Street, London N1 6NG
Tel: 020 7613 0743; Fax: 020 7613 5280
Another organisation promoting a wide variety of ways to reduce the
environmental impact of getting around.

Trees for Life
The Park, Findhorn Bay, Forres, IV36 3TZ
Tel: 01309 691292; Fax: 01309 691155; e-mail: trees@findhorn.org
Website: www.treesforlife.org.uk
Environmental charity aiming to restore the native Caledonian Forest
in the Scottish Highlands. Volunteer work weeks available.

The Vegan Society
7 Battle Road, St Leonard's-on-Sea, East Sussex, TN37 7AA
Tel: 01424 427393
Website: www.vegansociety.com
Produces a quarterly magazine, as well information sheets and
publications such as *Animal Free Shopper* and *Vegan Travel Guide*.

The Vegetarian Society
Parkdale, Dunham Road, Altrincham, Cheshire, WA14 4QG
Tel: 0161 928 0793
Website: www.vegsoc.org

Vinceremos
261 Upper Town Street, Leeds, LS13 3JT
Tel: 0113 257 7545; Fax: 0113 257 6906
Website: vinceremos@aol.com
Organic wine importers and mail order suppliers.

Waste Watch
Europe House, Ground Floor, 13–17 Ironmonger Row, London
EC1V 3QG. Tel: 020 7253 6266
Website: www.wastewatch.org.uk
Promotes action on waste reduction and recycling.

What Doctors Don't Tell You
Freephone: 0800 146054
Website: www.wddty.co.uk
Monthly magazine which aims to tell the whole truth about modern
medicine with discussion of alternative views.

The Women's Environmental Network (WEN)
87 Worship Street, London EC2A 2BE
Tel: 020 7247 3327; Fax: 020 7247 4740
Website: www.gn.apc.org/wen
Membership organisation that campaigns on a range of
environmental issues of particular concern to women. Leaflets on
many topics.

Eco Living

Willing Workers on Organic Farms (WWOOF)
PO Box 2675, Lewes, East Sussex, BN7 1RB
Website: www.wwf-uk.org
It costs £10 to join, then all board and lodging is free on the farms
where you work.

Index